Manifest Your Future

Design Your Life!

DENNIS A. BELANGER

BALBOA.PRESS
A DIVISION OF HAY HOUSE

This book is a work of non-fiction. Unless otherwise noted, the author and the publisher make no explicit guarantees as to the accuracy of the information contained in this book and in some cases, names of people and places have been altered to protect their privacy.

Balboa Press books may be ordered through booksellers or by contacting:

Balboa Press
A Division of Hay House
1663 Liberty Drive
Bloomington, IN 47403
www.balboapress.com
844-682-1282

Because of the dynamic nature of the Internet, any web addresses or links contained in this book may have changed since publication and may no longer be valid. The views expressed in this work are solely those of the author and do not necessarily reflect the views of the publisher, and the publisher hereby disclaims any responsibility for them.

The author of this book does not dispense medical advice or prescribe the use of any technique as a form of treatment for physical, emotional, or medical problems without the advice of a physician, either directly or indirectly. The intent of the author is only to offer information of a general nature to help you in your quest for emotional and spiritual well-being. In the event you use any of the information in this book for yourself, which is your constitutional right, the author and the publisher assume no responsibility for your actions.

Any people depicted in stock imagery provided by Getty Images are models, and such images are being used for illustrative purposes only. Certain stock imagery © Getty Images.

Print information available on the last page.

ISBN: 978-1-9822-7260-9 (sc)
ISBN: 978-1-9822-7259-3 (hc)
ISBN: 978-1-9822-7258-6 (e)

Library of Congress Control Number: 2021915864

Balboa Press rev. date: 08/30/2021

Contents

Preface

My wish is to assist people in finding a better quality of life through understanding of the Self, and achieving self-realization.

Discovering that there is a path to joy and happiness, and that this comes only after discovering and experiencing your true inner-self, healing as needed, and then projecting outward from the center of your true self, is a beautiful thing. When you interact with the universe, which is explained in this book in a step-by-step process, a sense of true belonging and connectedness will become the base that you operate from. Practice will bring further refinement; then, you can share your knowledge with others. Discovering the center of your true self is the key. I hope you will find this book useful in facilitating your personal journey to happiness, fulfillment, and manifesting all that you want.

Let's take a moment and think of having a computer program that doesn't work very well. Maybe it crashes on occasion, or even regularly. Maybe it doesn't do everything you need it to do. Now if this is the case, and you can identify with this, either you can live with the current performance and experience the identical performance continuously or you can go inside and rewrite the internal code, test it, and continue on your way until you've reached your desired performance or destination.

The information presented here is your opportunity, a road map if you will, to get you to the destination of your choosing. You must do the work though. Simply reading this book and not engaging in the internal work will not produce the desired outcome. Only by making this "your" personal and ardent journey – a journey of investigation and discovery – can any knowledge and understanding be gained. So do the exercises, search internally to the far reaches, enjoy the discovery of your true self, evolve into a much higher state of being, and enjoy all that you create.

This book will cover many things, but my primary focus is on how we can all go to our connected Center, which is where self-realization, self-healing, and self-manifesting take place. Not only will I discuss the conceptual ideas, but also offer time-tested exercises for you to experience this most personal journey for yourself.

When you read something that pertains specifically to you, take a moment and write it in the appendix section of this book, titled "Action Steps I Promise to Take, Practice, and Master". In doing so you will create your own personal step-by-step action plan. This will lead your evolution of consciousness and being to the exact place where you envision yourself in the future.

The information in this book comes from my life's observations, personal practices and experiences, as well as from extensive reading of the many scholars and visionaries I have had the good fortune to learn from. I know it has helped me and many others. I hope you will find this to be valuable as well.

Acknowledgements

To Beth – The Love of my life, my wife, and the person who reenergized and expanded my spiritual practice by co-creating a journey with many hardly-believable self-manifestations, that seemed to act as guideposts for me to write this book. It was with the many late night talks and cups of tea that I further developed and finalized the practice that is now explained in this book.

And to Yiannis Gianareas, my good friend for life, for our late night spiritual talks and additional exposure to esoteric spiritual laws that were previously unknown to me. Reading books on spirituality gave me the conceptual teachings I needed. Seeing someone living the conceptual teachings from the core of their being enabled me to cross over the line from conceptual thinking to actively manifesting reality.

Additionally, I would like to thank my good friends Audrey and Josh Vangrove, Kim Johnson and Darlene Wagner, for their valuable contributions with editing and feedback.

Life is such a wonderful trip; I'm so glad you are all a part of it.

Observational Understanding

Beautiful Connected Innocence

When you were born, you were beautiful, innocent, and closely connected to the most basic, and also the most precious, thing in life – Love. Starting from this Beautiful Connected Innocence, you begin the journey of experiencing and learning, experiencing and learning, and experiencing and learning.

The positive, as well as the negative experiences we have, and our reaction to them, will have a large part in sculpting our view of the world, and more specifically, our place in it.

We sometimes absorb the negative things that were either said to us or done to us, from seemingly authoritative figures, who in reality have no authority to govern our lives at all. It could be our third grade teacher, a neighbor or family friend, older kids at school, or even one or both of our parents. During the earliest part of our life, we are shaped by what is handed to us. In the later part of our life, we must learn to sort through the past, use the lessons we value and discard the experiences and the concepts that no longer serve us beneficially. We need to do this in order to create and manifest exactly how we want the rest of our lives to be.

If we store any early incorrect information and use it to form part of our basic identity, it can alter and change the normal course of our life. If we live our life with even the smallest amount of fear or self-doubt, our choices are likely to be negatively affected.

This sometimes remains undetected entirely, or we may have a hint of something that's really deep inside that we choose to easily dismiss or ignore. Sometimes we repeat the same destructive patterns and just throw our hands in the air and call it fate. Other times we know what it is, and we think we just have to live with it. Then we suffer the consequences not knowing that there is a way to change by altering and enhancing our perception.

By knowing the steps needed to manifest the life you wish to live you will be free to create and experience the future as you envision it. With practice and introspection as outlined in this book, so long as you do the needed work, you can actually manifest the positive changes you want to achieve.

It is not my intention to represent myself as a trained or licensed professional, but rather as an awakened person who has been on this path and has helped others in their own personal search. If you feel like you need professional help, please seek it. If you feel like learning about self-discovery and creating your future world, please read on. I don't believe anyone can become fully realized or reach any level of self-realization unless these implanted negative thoughts are discovered and dealt with. The place to deal with them is in your Universally Connected Center, which we will learn more about in the coming chapters. This is a unique and personal journey and one that is well worth taking. It is yours, and yours alone, to take.

We all know to some degree that we are spiritual beings. If we are all Spiritual Beings, then, where did we come from?

In this excerpt from Rabindranath Tagore's beautiful poem called *The Beginning*, in which a baby is asking its mother: "Where did I come from?" Tagore touches on the idea of universal connectedness:

"Heaven's first darling, twin-born with the morning light, you have floated down the stream of the world's life, and at last you have stranded on my heart.

As I gaze on your face, mystery overwhelms me; you who belong to all have become mine.

For fear of losing you I hold you tight to my breast.

What magic has snared the world's treasure in these slender arms of mine?"

Isn't this a beautiful and intriguing expression? "You who belong to all, have become mine" doesn't negate the fact that you still belong to all, and by association, are still connected to all. It is where you came from and where you will return to. This is true for every one of us without exception. This is who you are at the most fundamental level. Everything that has been layered on top of this are only adjustments and additions. However treacherous your journey may have been, or might be at times, it always has the potential to be a wondrous and joyful journey full of creation. It is extremely important to acknowledge that you have always been, and still are, connected to the All in the universe.

This should be your basis for living, as well as your north star.

"As for the future, your task is not to foresee it, but to enable it."

~ Antoine de Saint-Exupery

Understanding the Flow

The path to Beautiful Centered Living is sometimes interrupted by negative events that happen to us as we travel through this lifetime. These are the things that we can overcome and correct so that we can have a better life filled with love, happiness, and the accomplishment of our dreams.

As we grow older, and leave the infantile stage, we all encounter societal programming and autonomic conditioning. This is society's way of training us to adapt into the normal and accepted behaviors that have been deemed respectable by the existing group in the established society. Much of this is good but some of it is not, or at the very least, has become outdated. Anything that alters your path to happiness and fulfillment, or limits who you are or who you want to become, should be recognized as something that needs to be changed. Interestingly, the Greek philosopher, Heraclitus said: "Change is the only constant in life." So let us embrace this truth for what it is, and realize we have the power to create any future change we desire.

Joseph Campbell, in his book *The Hero with a Thousand Faces* explains that the person (the Hero) that begins the change process is usually considered by many to be an outcast or rebel, a "freak" of society who just can't go along with the status quo. This outcast is actually the savior of society as he or she brings the rest of society to a more evolved understanding and to a higher order of being. Think of the early woman's suffrage movement, the civil rights movement, gay marriage and equality, and now, more recently, the Black Lives Matter movement. All of these movements took the heat at first, then moved society to a much needed and more highly evolved state, and I believe we are (and will be) far better off for it – individually and collectively.

Once we understand 'what things' we have encountered that need to be changed (and more on this shortly), we start to think, see, and experience cracks in the old self that are starting to open. And this is good, it's how the light gets in. This is the fuel needed for future growth. We may not fully understand the process right away, but rather have a sense that something in our personal life is about to evolve into a higher and more enlightened state. As we glimpse into the mystery, an increased wakefulness begins to stir, our connectedness becomes apparent, and we begin to manifest our new higher order of being.

Once we grasp what we need to change and make the determination that now is the right time to take the needed steps, often times we find a resistance to the very change we want to realize. This can come not only from the outside, but also from deep within ourselves. These are the Dragons that we keep locked away deep within our psyche. Letting these Dragons affect us on a somewhat continual basis are the main causes of all the negative events in our lives.

Our Dragons come from societal programming and autonomic conditioning. We've been thoroughly trained to create the life we are experiencing, be it negative or positive – if we started from a clean slate, there is no other way it could have happened! In addition, we will continue to create positive or negative events based on the power and acceptance we give to these Dragons.

If we choose to use the beneficial input and guidance that comes from our own Spiritual Center, rather than rely on the information handed to us by others, our future can be drastically improved.

Negative or limiting beliefs that may have been programmed into us may be something like "Oh, you can't do that." and "What do you think you're doing?" "You're not good enough." (i.e. get back into your proper place). This can keep us frozen in place for years!

Just listen to the self-talk that echoes inside your head every day. This will reveal what your past programming has been. These thoughts reinforce the same theme almost constantly, and often times go completely unnoticed. This will tell you how you've been auto-programmed, and it has likely been that way for an extremely long time. If you want to know what's creating the events in your life, you just found it.

The final blockades that often keep us from reaching our true desire and destiny are fear and doubt. These can be deeply, deeply rooted in our psyche. This is what limits us and prevents us from creating the life we want to have. What would you attempt if you knew you could not fail? How would your current and future life be different if you were confident you would succeed at everything you attempted? By overcoming these blockages, you are opening the way for new growth. This is what's needed to become successful.

If you have had times in your life where it seemed like it was really difficult to move forward, the fear that you keep inside is likely what has kept you from progressing. These fears are born from, and are a result of, our created Dragons (created by ourselves often times with the help of others).

Finding our Dragons and slaying them is what releases the negative conditioning of the previous programming, and the fear that results from them. This propels us forward on our evolutionary path, uninhibited, so we can reach our state of Beautiful Centered Living.

> *"When traveling on a road, there must be an end; but when astray, your wanderings are limitless."*
>
> ~ Seneca

Glimpsing Into the Mystery

For most of us, thinking about our spiritual journey begins when we start to wonder if there is something more and have the feeling that life is somehow incomplete…like there is something missing. We start looking for alternative answers – wondering gives way to searching; searching gives way to glimpsing the truth; glimpsing the truth gives way to experiencing the truth; experiencing the truth gives way to actively manifesting; and this gives way to teaching others.

There are only two possible reasons why a person would not benefit from doing this work: not beginning and not sufficiently finishing.

When you choose to begin your journey you will have the universe working with you, and this will open new doors and create a life more fulfilling and rewarding than you could have ever imagined.

"The experience of mystery comes not from expecting it but through yielding all your programs, because your programs are based on fear and desire. Drop them and the radiance comes."

~ Joseph Campbell
Thou Art That, Transforming Religious Metaphor

You get to Choose

Anyone can be a teacher. We all learn from each other. It's through cooperation and learning that we grow and our prosperity increases.

There are other individuals who are not as far along on the spiritual path as you are, and they can learn some things from you. Others may be further along the path than we are, and we can all certainly learn from them.

In our daily interactions, opportunities to learn come to us all the time. Arrogance will keep us closed rather than open, and inaction will keep us locked up in the same box in which we never seem to evolve.

To be actively participating in life is to be open to the world and everything that is participating in it, living fluidly, and embracing the ever-evolving changes that are constantly present. It's through cooperation that species thrive and flourish. By being involved in the world and its play of energy, you exercise your full participation and engagement. Each lifetime offers only a finite amount of time to live, learn, and love. You're the one who makes change happen and in doing so, you help mankind on its own evolutionary journey.

"If you want truth to stand clear before you, never be 'for' or 'against'. The struggle between 'for' and 'against' is the minds worst disease."

~ Sent-Ts'san C. 700 CE

Reflecting on this chapter, I invite you to write down any applicable thoughts, take-aways, or lightbulb moments that your inner-self is realizing and trying to communicate to you:

_____

_____

_____

_____

_____

_____

_____

_____

_____

_____

_____

_____

Societal Programming & Autonomic Conditioning

Looking in the Rear View Mirror

Societal programming and autonomic conditioning normally starts at a very young age. This is when the seeds of fear are first planted… when the "Should Do's" and "Shouldn't Do's" start to limit and cage you. Of course, most directives and instructions received from our parents are helpful (hopefully), but some are not…and they stick in our subconscious and become the Dragons we must slay later in life if we are to become fully self-realized, reach our full potential, and manifest our life's purpose. Just as it takes a village to raise a child, the entire village also joins in when it comes to creating societal programming and autonomic conditioning, to the possible detriment of the young child.

As described by John Bradshaw, in his book *Bradshaw on the Family*, many times this detrimental programming is multigenerational and the active participants aren't even aware of their harmful words or actions. I've seen this first-hand.

As an example, let's say a small child is verbally and emotionally abused, being called stupid, lazy, or unattractive. Additionally, that child hears almost constantly: "Why can't you be like your brother!" or, "Why can't you be like your sister!" So one sibling is 'golden boy' (or girl) and the other one is degraded for an entire lifetime.

Dennis A. Belanger

When the verbally and emotionally abused child grows up and has their own family, low and behold, there is one child that they "just can't get along with" and the same cycle repeats itself. One more beautiful and innocent life has been damaged or marginalized, possibly damaged for an entire lifetime. Worst yet, others from future generations may be in-line for very similar, if not identical, ill-treatment.

The need for love is ubiquitous. Sometimes it happens that the only way for a child to attain the love of one or both parents is to emulate their parents in adulthood, and this tendency often goes unnoticed by the individual. If this is the case, then multigenerational abuse can be generated, and not only has another soul been damaged, but likely many souls for generations to come. Awareness and intelligence is what's needed to overcome this and you have the potential to stop this pattern.

Some experience the need to have control over everything in their world – people, schedules, relationships, spouses, and children. They don't realize this only brings more isolation and loneliness – it never brings happiness. Once realized, the progression of this multigenerational dis-ease can be stopped, and wellness restored.

The first of The Four Noble Truths in Buddhism (although I'm not a Buddhist) identifies the existence of suffering in the world. It then goes on to explain that one of the root causes of suffering is ignorance. It pains me to think of how much suffering is self-inflicted and needlessly passed on to others, especially to small children, when the only real cause *is* ignorance (not knowing).

The good news is you can reverse these effects if this has happened to you or if you have experienced other traumas or were filled with limiting ideas that keep you from reaching your own self-realization and goals. Once you awaken to the truth about your ability to manifest and create your own reality, you are empowered. How to do this will be explained in the upcoming chapters.

10

*"I am not what happened to me, I am what I choose
to become. Your visions will become clear only when
you can look into your own heart. Who looks outside
dreams; who looks inside, awakes."*

~ Carl Jung

What Does Society Teach Us, and How?

If you think the amount of internal thoughts we bombard
ourselves with over years, decades, and lifetimes are staggering, add to
that all of the advertisements we see on TV, tons of pop-up computer
ads, direct mailings, and the directives we hear on the radio.

The amount of information we have coming at us is unprecedented
in human history. Everyone is telling us how we should live our life or
why we need to perform or conform. Most informational intrusions
are represented as problems we have, and they just happen to have
what we need to fix our problems. Now add to this the amount of
advice we receive from friends, co-workers, trained professionals, and
family, who have all been influenced by the same confusion.

Society also teaches us how to behave, as well as what is acceptable
and what is not. A lot of this information gets hardwired into our
psyche, and not all of it is beneficial. We all know the stereotypes
and images that are inflicted on the populace.

It's easy to look at other cultures and condemn their actions and
policies with total disregard for the fact that only a short time ago
we, here in the U.S., were guilty of genocide, slavery, the suppression
of personal freedoms for many, the disallowance of woman's rights,
dropping nuclear weapons on a population consisting of innocent
civilians, etc.

In 1920, the 19th amendment was ratified and women in the
United States finally got the right to vote, seventy years before that
it was unlawful for women to own property. The Emancipation
Proclamation was signed just over 150 years ago, and some could

argue successfully that it wasn't until the Civil Rights Act of 1964 that it got any teeth, and even currently one could argue successfully that there is still much work to be done to achieve what the Civil Rights Act set forth as law. My point here is that society doesn't always get it right, and sometimes (many times) society gets it extremely wrong.

Therefore, if we agree that we are bombarded with societal information, maybe we should look at how our internal pictures have been shaped and reshaped repeatedly on a micro and macro level. Are we designing our internal picture or has it been designed for us?

There can be no change in our self-image without the dissolution of the boundaries that constitute our self-image. When we dissolve these boundaries, we experience space. Space allows the self-image to loosen and change.

> *"When you're on a journey and the end keeps getting further and further away, then you realize that the real end is the journey."*
> ~ Karlfried Graf Durckheim

Reflecting on this chapter, I invite you to write down any applicable thoughts, take-aways, or lightbulb moments that your inner-self is realizing and trying to communicate to you:

_____

_____

_____

_____

_____

_____

_____

_____

_____

_____

_____

_____

Developing Spirituality

Spiritual Nature

I'm a big fan of reading every spiritual text that you can get your hands on, and that's every one of them, and why not? More information is better than less! Their core teachings are all very similar and best taken metaphorically rather than literally. In the Hindu Vedas, it says: "Truth is one; the sages call it by many names."

The idea of handing the outcome of your life over to another person, a higher power, God, religion, the Universe, your favorite Guru, or whatever, is another way of saying you will not take the journey that lies before you…"let someone else do it for me, and I'll see how *that* works".

Passing off the work that needs to be done by *you* generally doesn't get you anywhere. You may find some false comfort for a little while, but you don't end up going to where you know you want to be, should be, and deserve to be.

Religious teachings generally all say "Go outward." while most spiritual texts that the religions are based on, say "Go inward!" "The kingdom of Heaven is within you." (King James Bible/Luke 17:20-21) In this case, if you want to find Heaven, where should you go? It's obvious – within you!

Kneel, look up towards the sky and say your prayers – go outward – were among my early childhood Catholic teachings. Others kneel, face Mecca, and cast their prayers outward when they express their religious devotion, regardless of where they are on the planet. For me, the religious dogmas stopped making sense when I was fourteen years old, and my inward spiritual journey began.

Although I am not religious in any way, I do find that all *spiritual texts* have value when taken metaphorically, and have even more value when you see them as a collective set. When you take note that God is in me, you, and in everything, as per Christianity, and compare that with the meaning of Namaste – the Deity in me recognizes the Deity in you, as in the Hindu faith, you realize these spiritual teaching are not at odds with each other, they are saying the very same thing.

If we all have God Energy in us, why can't we all get along? Why do I need to prove you wrong, try to elevate my beliefs over yours, or lie and cast war upon you? Yet religions of all kinds – not spirituality – have been doing this ever since they first began.

Whenever I ask a very religious person if he or she is familiar with the other religious teachings, I usually get the same answer: "No, I don't need to; I have everything I need right in this book." If you take a step back and think about it, doesn't that seem limiting?

Spiritual teachings can be a great addition to your life if you interpret them for yourself metaphorically, rather than literally. It really is a great big beautiful world out there. Let's explore what's possible if we don't limit our knowledge, our thinking, or our potential experiences.

> *"It is not impermanence that makes us suffer. What makes us suffer is wanting things to be permanent when they are not."*
> – Thich Naht Hanh

Finding Your Spiritual Center

To find your Spiritual Center you will need to go inside, to the core of your being, which you will find is full of pure energy and connectedness. Meditation will definitely take you inward where you will cast off the external distractions and come to know your inner-self. Some of the earliest written records of meditation are from around 1500 BCE, and belong to the Hindu traditions. Meditation is still widely practiced by millions of people today. The four types of meditation I practice will be discussed in a later chapter.

When you get to the deepest levels of your subconscious, you can cast your intentions or ask the questions you need answers to, and you will see the results of your requests or inquiries fairly quickly, and in a very concrete way. We will talk about one style of meditation that focuses specifically on this, and you will be amazed at the outcomes that can be realized by using this technique, with just a small amount of practice.

It is from these inner levels of consciousness where your questions will be answered and your Dragons discovered and permanently dealt with. Their memories may still exist, but the power and influence they have in your life will be nullified.

As far as finding answers to deeply hidden questions, I'll share a very personal story: I went through a divorce where my ex-wife and my three kids moved about two hours away. This seemed like the best solution, as I needed to work many hours to cover the family expenses for two households and my ex-wife was more available to see the kids off to school and be there when they returned, plus all of the other activities and interactions that a parent needs to be there for on a daily basis.

I held the deep pain of not seeing my kids when I returned home to an empty house, and this was something that stuck with me like a dagger in my heart. When I did go to pick them up on weekends, just seeing them, and regardless of my joy at seeing them, I felt this deep and painful sorrow. I had linked the pain of losing them from my everyday life with seeing them. The healing solution came from an interesting exercise from someone in my life who was learning shamanism. This exercise connected me with my subconscious mind in a way I had never experienced before.

I was asked by the practitioner to think of a question I had difficulty finding an answer to, and just to hold that question quietly in my thoughts...just hold it, and put it off to the side for now. The facilitator who was performing the healing exercise was monotonously beating a drum (like at a drum circle) with one strike, then a pause, followed by three more consecutive strikes followed by a pause (bum...bum, bum, bum.... bum... bum, bum, bum...) and this would continue throughout the entire session. I was told to think of a place in nature that I knew fairly well, and was a place that I could relax and connect with nature.

I pictured myself on top of a mountain ridge that I knew well, laying under some mid-sized pines and furs, as I had actually done many times before. Then I was instructed to feel how the earth felt beneath my body, feel any stones, sticks or roots, and any unevenness in the earth, and I did. Feel the sun on your face, feel the warmth of the sun as the trees sway in and out, diffusing the sunlight's path to you; hear the sound of the breeze as it flows through the pines and the aspens as it makes its way towards you and then finally reaches you; feel the breeze as it crosses your body – just be there (bum... bum, bum, bum...bum...bum, bum, bum...).

After doing several repetitions of this, I was instructed to notice a person some distance away, and even though I couldn't tell at this point whether it was a friend or foe, I had nothing to worry about. (bum...bum, bum, bum...bum...bum, bum, bum...). A number of verbal repetitions as stated above followed, accompanied by the monotonous beat of the drum, which put me into a very unique state that allowed me to relax and go deeper and deeper into my own inner consciousness.

Then I was told to notice that the person I had seen in the distance was advancing in my direction and because of the distance that remained between us, I still couldn't determine if it was a friend or foe, but I had nothing to be concerned about, just notice he is coming your way and is getting closer. (bum...bum, bum, bum...bum...bum, bum, bum...) The repetitiveness of the verbal instructions along with the monotonous drum beat put me in a unique state of being, as I slipped closer and closer into the area of my subconscious, deeper and deeper inside did I go.

The approaching stranger continued to narrow the distance between him and I, until finally he was so close his identity could be known, and the facilitator said to me: "Oh, it's your subconscious; go ahead and ask your question." I did. I asked why do I have this sorrowful link and how do I resolve it – why do I feel this way? The answers flowed almost faster than I could comprehend and process the information and 98% of the unwanted link was dissolved, and the remaining 2% dissolved quickly thereafter on its own. It was truly an amazing experience.

As you will see, there are many ways to reach your Spiritual Center and this is a truly amazing and powerful place. Connecting with the "All" on a regular basis is the best way to cast your desired intentions to the Connectedness that we all share. By practicing techniques that take you to your Center, and there are many to choose from, your ability to manifest will make you understand how the world, and universe, actually work.

When in a state of meditation, and in the area where the conscious mind gives way to your Spiritual Center, you can communicate your intentions outwardly and manifest the things you desire most. I find it best to not only say what your intention is, but also to add the reason why you want the desired outcome, as well as what you will do once you have manifested the reality you are asking for.

This focuses your intention and increases the power attached to it. If someone asked me for a certain sum of money with no reason or explanation given, I would be more likely to say no. If that same person asked me for the same sum of money, and added that it was for this really good cause, and they had already organized a number of volunteers in the community who were committed to this project, and once complete, the world will be a better place, then I would very likely support their cause and join forces with them. You'll find our Universe works the same way.

What you can manifest from your subconscious realm with just a little practice is truly amazing.

> *"We are Spirit and Soul, not body and brain. The Soul has no sex, no hormones, no biological tendencies. The Soul is pure, loving energy."*
> ~ Brian Weiss, M.D., Messages from the Masters

Meditation Basics

I've been asked: "Is meditation a doorway or a gateway?" My answer is always the same: "No. Meditation is what takes you through the doorway, and through the gateway."

If meditation takes you through the doorway and through the gateway, then where do you go?

You go into the core of your spiritual being. And from here, you have many options.

If you are new to meditation, first realize that meditation is as natural as breathing. In fact, breathing techniques are an important aspect to achieving a meditative state.

You always want to breathe in through your nostrils and exhale through your mouth. You also want complete breaths – breath in until you can't comfortably breathe in anymore and exhale until every bit of breath has exited your body.

On your inhale, first extend your belly activating your diaphragm, and then expand the chest, completely filling your lungs with breath. On your exhale, empty the lungs by contracting your chest first, then contract your belly to relax the diaphragm and complete the exhale. If at first you find this method distracting, breathe simultaneously with your chest and your belly, and move to this technique as you become more advanced and comfortable in your practice.

In addition, you should find a comfortable place to sit, either in a cross-leg position, in a Lotus pose where each foot is placed on the opposite thigh, or in a comfortable chair. If choosing the cross-leg or Lotus pose, sitting on the edge of a meditation cushion or folded towel will help keep your spine erect and make the pose more comfortable. You can also lie down on a comfortable mattress without a pillow under your head. This will keep your posture correct while you are in a prone position.

When in the sitting position, your hands should rest on top of your thighs with your palms facing upwards. You can connect the tip of your first or second finger with the tip of your thumb to form a circle.

Your space should be quiet and serene. Either a salt lamp, safely lit candle, or other soft and dim lighting, as well as comfortable clothing, will make your meditation practice more enjoyable.

The whole idea and purpose of meditation is to quiet the mind. Once you have totally quieted the mind, you will begin to experience your true self.

> *"Who am I? Am I the bulb that carries the light, or am*
> *I the light of which the bulb is the vehicle?"*
> ~ Joseph Campbell, The Power of Myth

Different Styles of Meditation

I like to divide the various styles of meditation into two camps: passive and active, or non-participatory and participatory. Passive or non-participatory meditation, like a relaxing meditation brought on by listening to meditative music or Transcendental Meditation (TM) will allow you to experience your internal bliss, uninterrupted by anything. In this state of being, you are accessing your subconscious mind and blocking out the conscious mind. This is a very important part of learning and should be practiced initially until a certain level of proficiency has been reached. When you are feeling comfortable with your level of achievement and have a desire to seek answers or manifest and create what you want to experience in your life, you can begin the practice of active or participatory meditation.

Active or participatory meditation is when you engage both your conscious and subconscious mind at the same time in a focused, self-guided meditation, with the intention of bringing about a planned result. These styles are best used when you have a difficult question and want to tap into the universal consciousness to gain insight, or when you want to cast your intentions into the universal consciousness for the purpose of creation and manifestation.

To accomplish this, first concentrate on your question or on the meaningful intention you wish to manifest, and once firmly in place, set it aside temporarily. Then use the passive, non-participatory meditation techniques you've developed to guide you into your inner-self, which is your subconscious mind (also your Spiritual Center). This connects you to the collective (universal) consciousness. When you feel the time is appropriate, you can cross over from your subconscious mind and retrieve your question or intention from your conscious mind, and return with it into your subconscious mind. This will connect your question or intention to manifest, with the greater universal source of intelligence and creation that we are all connected to.

Every time you are truly connected to any of these meditative states you are truly connected to all that is, has been, and will be.

> *"When people go within and connect with themselves,*
> *they realize they are connected to the universe and they*
> *are connected to all living things."*
> ~ Armand DiMele

Transcendental Meditation

I started meditating when I was fourteen years old, after coming across a paperback book that explained the technique of Transcendental Meditation (TM). I have used this method continuously, in some periods of my life more regularly than others, although never with a long break from practice. Meditation *is* the way inward. And please understand that before anything manifests, it already exists in our world in its un-manifested state.

The purpose of TM is to transcend thought itself and to reach a state of pure awareness, which is what I have referred to previously as you going to your Spiritual Center. From this place, you can experience the peaceful connectedness that the quieted mind actualizes when in meditation. A feeling of serenity, subtle energy, and a sense of being connected to all things can be easily achieved with just a small amount of regular practice. Once proficient in TM, you'll have control over the mind and all other forms of meditation will be enhanced.

When you are in a transcendental meditative state you are everywhere and nowhere at the same time.

I think the biggest benefit from meditation is feeling the energy that you have inside yourself and knowing that you *really are* this energy. This is the same energy that is omnipresent and makes up everything in the universe. We are all made from the same energy whether it is stored as mass ($E=MC^2$) or any one of the various waves in the electromagnetic spectrum – it's all energy and we are not at all separate from it.

To experience TM, start by sitting comfortably on a small cushion with your legs crossed meditation style and your back vertically straight. By sitting on the edge of the cushion rather than squarely on top of it, you will tilt your pelvis slightly forward, making it easier to sit comfortably in an erect position. While internally focusing on your third eye (the space between your eyebrows), breathe in deeply through your nose, completely filling your lungs by first expanding your belly, then your chest. Hold for just a second and gently exhale through your mouth evenly and steadily until every bit of breath has been completely exhaled from your lungs. Pause slightly, and again gently begin the inhale breath through your nose until your lungs are comfortably full, and exhale as before. Repeat these steps until you feel your mind has quieted sufficiently and a blissful state is achieved. Once you start your practice, you will easily know when this is.

Placing a safely lit candle approximately four feet from where you are sitting can also be helpful. With this slightly different technique, you can look into the very center of the flame. Notice the various colors that make up the flame and how it dances at the very slightest movement of the surrounding air. Do this without any active thought, just be aware of what you are experiencing and you will feel yourself becoming one with your surroundings. Understand that you and the flame are fundamentally the same thing. You are connected to this just as you are connected to all things. This will quiet your mind, eliminate the constant chatter normally experienced in daily life, and put you in touch with the bliss that is at the most elemental part of reality. At this point – just experience your true nature and feel the connection you have with this universal energy.

Once you've reached the level of meditation you want, stay relaxed and breathe however your body wants to. You may occasionally encounter a wandering mind with extraneous thoughts appearing randomly. You can just tell your conscious mind – No! This will allow you the opportunity to gain control over your conscious mind and you will soon become the master of it. A few additional deep breaths may also be helpful to quiet the wandering mind.

The conscious mind has been likened to a rambunctious child who can be told to sit still to no avail. After repeatedly being told to sit still, eventually the child will realize there is no other choice than to obey the directive. Your wandering mind is very similar. Anytime any vagarious thoughts try to enter your mind, just repeat the same command – No! Once it becomes clear that your instruction must be followed, your mind will stop the chatter and do what has been asked.

You can also follow your breath with your awareness as you breathe in and breathe out. You can do this by just watching your in-breath and your out-breath, and seeing it as a soft light or as pure energy. This focusing will also pacify the mind.

I have often repeated the mantra AUM (also known as OM). Interestingly, AUM is known as the four-syllable word, the A, U, M, are the three obvious syllables, and the fourth syllable is the silence between each mantra, from which everything comes, and to which everything returns back into.

While studying Eckankar many years ago, we used to chant the word HU (pronounced HEW) for the entire exhalation of each breath. This is reportedly an ancient name for God, which is another name for universal (omnipresent) energy. It does offer a slightly different vibration, and although I personally prefer AUM, it may be something you want to try for yourself. Just remember, every mantra has its own vibration, and is about going inward on your very own personal journey.

Using these or any other vibrational mantras that are more fitting to you personally, is another option to stop the chatter of the mind, which the Buddhists refer to as monkey-mind, and let you experience yourself on a profoundly deeper level. It will only take a small amount of regular daily practice for you to become extremely proficient at realizing your Spiritual Center.

Spatial Meditation

I currently practice this almost every day in the morning before I rise and in the evening before I go to sleep.

We talked about how to get to your Spiritual Center, once there you can use Spatial Meditation to empower the launching of your intentions from your Spiritual Center to the universal field of energy. This will bring about the changes you wish to manifest into your life. You may have heard someone say, "Just put it out there." I assure you that this is where *you want to be* to express and launch your intentions to the universe. It works extremely well and I've never known anything more demonstratively powerful.

To experience this for yourself, first determine what it is that you want to manifest, or what question you would like answered. Then lie down comfortably in a quiet place – a comfortable mattress without a pillow in a quiet bedroom works well as it will keep you comfortable and in proper postural alignment.

Start by taking about ten complete breaths – but don't actually count – just take enough deep breaths to get you to your Spiritual Center. You should breathe just like in the practice of Transcendental Meditation, steadily in through the nose and exhale gently through the mouth. It should take you approximately fifteen seconds to inhale and fifteen seconds on the exhale.

For this meditation, you will be placing your awareness at various locations throughout your body for approximately ten seconds at each location. Again, don't use your mind to count, just feel it with your being and allow your "self" to determine when you've concentrated your awareness sufficiently in that area, then move to the next location. The amount of time is less important than your experiencing the concentrated placement of your attention. Keep your awareness on the area until you can feel it in its concentrated form. You will energetically know when it is time to move to the next area.

Once you have reached your quieted state, you will feel your conscious energy (awareness, attention). Now move your consciousness and awareness to the area of your third eye, between your eyebrows. When your awareness is firmly in place, feel it there (for approximately ten seconds). Now split your attention so that you put it on both temples at the same time and hold it there. Now move your awareness to your pituitary gland, which is located behind the bridge of your nose and between the ears. This gland is often called the master gland because it controls many other hormone glands, including the adrenals, the thyroid, and the reproductive organs. Now move your attention to the center of your lower jaw, feel your concentrated energy, then move your energy (your awareness) to back of your throat.

Now fill the entire space that is inside your skull, and after ten seconds move to the right outer surface of your skull. Now extend your consciousness to a place that is approximately twelve inches away from the right side of your skull, as this will extend out about halfway into the electromagnetic field that surrounds the human body, commonly referred to as your auric field.

Feel how you can move and project your energy and consciousness at will. (An advanced step is to extend your awareness further in all directions to a distance of 48 inches from the surface of your skin. This will permeate your entire auric field out to its final layer and you will benefit from a higher spiritual connection. This can also help protect you from the negative outside influences that may occasionally try to penetrate your energy field. You can work up to this level as you advance in your practice.)

Now bring your attention to the last position held at the right outer surface of your skull, and now to the vertical center of your skull. Hold each location until you feel the concentrated energy saturate the area, then move on to the next location.

Repeat to the left side by first focusing on the outer left surface of your skull, then twelve inches outside and away, back to the outer left surface of the skull, and back to the vertical center. Project now to an area twelve inches above your face, then sweep your energy through your skull and let it rest twelve inches beneath the back of your head.

Now move your attention into the area of your neck, feel it fill the neck area and expand slightly outward. Now slide your consciousness into your shoulders, now down the left arm and into your left hand and connect to the earth, however far away that may be. You can collect energy from the earth or distribute it to the earth – try both to get a feel for this beneficial exchange of energy and to determine what is most needed.

After approximately ten seconds, feel your energy move upward through your left arm, cross your shoulders, and down through your right arm with the energy exiting out through your hand and again connecting with the earth. When you're comfortable and ready to move on, return your consciousness back to your shoulders and then into your chest. Once you feel your consciousness sufficiently fill your chest, move on to your abdomen, where your internal organs will become energized by your conscious energy. Then let your conscious energy flow into your hips, your right thigh, knee, right calf, right ankle, and right foot – taking approximately ten seconds at each location. Feel the energy exit through your right foot and connect again with the earth, exchanging energy in both directions. Then let the energy travel slowly back up the right leg, cross the hips, and down the left leg using the same process until you are grounding your left foot with the earth. When complete, bring your conscious energy slowly back to the hips.

The next step is to combine larger areas of the body, so connect the hips and both legs and feet, and feel the energy permeate this part of the body all at once and as one unit. After ten seconds, let this energy slide up and into your torso – from the shoulders to the hips and including both arms. Experience this for approximately ten seconds. Now let your consciousness flow to the neck and head as one unit. At this point, you will be very aware of the energy in your body and feel it as a vibrating energy. We do have a few more steps to take to experience an even more enlightened state.

Now combine the energy in the upper half of your body, from the tip of your head to your waist as one unit, and hold for ten seconds. Now combine the energy in your entire body, from the tip of your head to the bottoms of your feet, all as one unit. Feel this awakened energy permeate your entire body. This *is* your energetic self – your own cosmic energy – that you have awakened!

Once you have reached this level, lift your energy in its entirety so that it is twelve inches above your body, then twelve inches below, then twelve inches to the right, and then twelve inches to the left of your body…twelve inches above your head, now twelve inches below your feet. Now bring it back to center and experience the vibrancy of your Spiritual Center, alive with all its grandeur. Lastly, from your energetic center, expand your conscious awareness outwardly in all directions for a distance of twelve inches, and then bring it back to center.

Now is the time to cast your intentions that you want to

manifest, or to ask your question you are requesting an answer to. You should release them to the universe from this state of being and just let it be. Don't force anything or overwork at trying to get an answer, just let the universe work in its own divine way.

Answers to your questions will come shortly or within a few days. Be watchful as thoughts or events present themselves. Communication is sometimes delivered in subtle ways.

The answer might come to you when you least expect it. It could be something said by a stranger regarding a different situation or overhearing something from another conversation, or while dreaming. Your reticular activating system will be on high alert and catching signals from many sources. So do be aware of all the communications that manifest and be cognizant of how they apply to you.

Outcomes may be within a few days, a few weeks, or in some cases a few months if you're working on a larger manifestation with many events needing to come together. The universe knows when the best timing is, and we need to be patient and let the universe unfold as it should.,

Practicing this meditation once or twice daily, until you have received your answer or manifestation, will bring you definite results.

If you combine your practice with another person who is vibrating with you in a harmonious and synergistic way, you will realize an increased amplitude for your efforts. Beth and I do this anytime we have a larger manifestation we want to bring about, and it works beautifully.

With practice, your ability to connect and your increased knowledge of the power of intention will bring you to your natural state of creating. This has always existed within you, in your higher consciousness.

When you release your intentions to the universe from your Spiritual Center and take the necessary actions toward the outcome you are projecting, you will manifest many things that are almost unexplainable...I mean you will really question how this could have come to you so perfectly! In time, you will realize that it is in fact – YOU, as part of the totality of the universe – who are doing the creating. This is the most powerful way to create all the aspects of the life you want to experience.

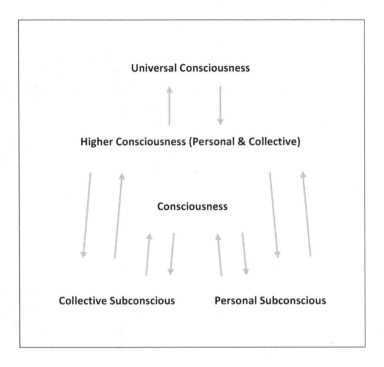

Chakra Meditation

Once you have experienced the connectedness and energy flow that come from practicing Transcendental Meditation and Spatial Meditation, you can use the same technique to awaken the energy stored in your chakras. Breathe as deeply and slowly as you choose, as directed by your inner self, throughout this meditation.

The energy in all chakras spin, and can spin in either direction. They are also like a flower facing upwards, rather than facing frontward or backward.

Let your inner self be your guide and choose whatever direction feels best. I suggest feeling the energy spin in one direction for a short time, then try the other direction for the same duration, and you will know what feels best for you or more like what you need. Just like being right-handed or left-handed, either is perfectly fine, and your choice will depend on your personal disposition.

Get to your Spiritual Center using TM or the Spatial Meditation techniques, and then focus on your Root Chakra, which is located at the base of the spine. Moving your energy around the area of each chakra will help you feel where its exact location is.

The Root Chakra grounds and connects us to the earth and stores of our cosmic energy can be released through the practice of Kundalini yoga.

See and feel a soft red light moving energetically through this area, letting go of anything you've been holding onto or storing in this area that is no longer serving you. Feel how you, through your Root Chakra, are connected to everything. Feel your conscious energy radiate from this energy center outward in all directions, first grounding yourself into the earth and then connecting to the infinite – first one, then the other, then both at the same time. Now feel the universal energy flowing from the earth and the infinite back into your Root Chakra and filling it with the pure energy coming from the All, which is the womb of creation. Know you are connected to everything and belong to everything, and everything is connected and belongs to you. Let go of everything and just feel your energetic connections. You have nothing to prove, only to be. Learn. You are on the path of discovering the truth of who you really are and what the universe is really made of.

Now move to your Sacral Chakra located in the upper part of the sacrum, just below the navel. The Sacral Chakra influences creativity and sexual energies. See and feel the color orange and the energy that resides here, and let it flow through you, connecting you to both Mother Earth and the infinite energy in the universe, just as you did with the previous chakra. Now connect your Sacral Chakra to your Root Chakra and feel your first two chakras connect and communicate in a spiral pattern. Again, let go of everything and just be.

Focus now on your third chakra, the Solar Plexus Chakra, located at the sternum. This chakra allows your authentic self to shine, and enables you to unleash your unlimited potential and transform your thoughts into action. Clearing and connecting this energy center to the infinite energy will build your personal power, your self-esteem, and your confidence. Feel and see the color yellow resting in your energy center like a glowing sun. Now feel this energy flowing downward and connecting deeply within the earth, then upwards into all points in the universe. All energy is connected. Become connected with this energy. Now feel your first three chakras connect and exchange life's energy in a spirally connected flow. Let all three vibrate evenly together.

Now move your consciousness to your Heart Chakra, located in the area of your heart at the center of your chest. The Heart Chakra is associated with compassion, serenity and the ability to love. Picture a bright, light green energy permeating through this energy center. Once you experience the energy in this chakra, let it expand outward into the universe until you feel sufficiently connected. Then let your energy connect with the deepest part of the earth. Now extend in both directions and feel with your full awareness your connectivity to everything. Now connect your Heart Chakra with the first three chakras and feel your connected energy flow freely within your first four chakras.

Next, bring your conscious energy to your Throat Chakra, located at the base of your throat. Balancing your Throat Chakra will increase your ability to communicate with others. Picture a turquoise-blue color energetically emanating from this area. Now connect, as with all the other chakras, to the earth below and the universe above. See and feel this exchange of energy and feel it flowing in both directions. Always let your inner self be your guide. Now connect this fifth chakra to the first four lower chakras – see and feel the energy flowing evenly, with the pathway being spiral in whichever direction feels most natural to you. Now feel your body vibrate as your awakened energy moves freely.

Your Third Eye Chakra is known as being the center for clarity, intuition, and foresight. It is located on the forehead, between your eyebrows. This is an important energy center for all meditation, and focusing on this energy center will always bring you back to a centered place. Feel the vibration of a deep blue color and see this color as it slowly spins. Now let it drop down into the earth and connect with the deepest part of the earth. Keep that connection and expand your consciousness upward. Now expand it to your right side, then your left. You are becoming proficient at moving your energy at will and this will stretch the walls that normally keep your energy confined and stifled. Now connect to all other lower energy centers as before. This is the energy that's within you and, in fact, is you. Feel the balanced connection between all the six chakras you have opened and exercised.

The seventh chakra is known as the Crown Chakra, and is located on the soft spot on the top of the head. This chakra connects you to infinite wisdom, greater understanding, and unity with higher consciousness. The energetic color that flows through this chakra is either bright white or an intense violet. Picture and feel both colors and choose what feels correct for you.

Move your conscious energy as you have with the other chakras, but now as you connect this chakra with all of the other chakras, feel the flow of energy coming from both Mother Earth below and the Infinite Universe above, and let this energy permeate all connected chakras. You are now fully grounded as well as connected to the source of everything.

When all of your normal guarding mechanisms are completely dismantled, and you are in touch with your innermost being, which is also, as said earlier, the womb of creation. You are now operating in the spiritual realm. This is the very same energy that is running through all things in creation! Now, you are not only with the divine, you realize that you are and always have been the divine!

You are connected with, and part of, "the All" and from here all creation and healing is possible. This is the completion of your total connection with reality – it goes beyond feminine and masculine, beyond the completing of Yin/Yang. Cast out your intentions or ask for answers from this connected state, or just be and realize your connection to everything that exists.

If you feel that a particular chakra is more difficult to experience or less responsive than others, this indicates a likely and potential blockage. Working with this chakra independently, both physically through massage or yoga, or spiritually through meditation and visualization, will loosen this blockage and the chakra will be restored to its natural condition. Practicing this Chakra Meditation on a regular basis will open your pathways simply by exercising and strengthening the energy flow within your body.

Another way to open your chakras is to work with the underlying cause of the blockage. If you feel that you're not grounded properly and your root chakra needs to open, practice grounding yourself by meditating in nature and visualize your connection to the earth. If you feel your heart chakra needs to open more, practice being more compassionate towards others. If it's your throat chakra that you want to open, practice speaking up for yourself and utilizing your voice more such as singing in the shower and verbalizing your thoughts freely to others when appropriate.

Other physical practices such as Pingshuai Gong, by Qi Gong master Lee Feng San, will help move energy through the body thereby dissipating any energy blockages.

The first three chakras are known to be elemental, instinctual, and animalistic as compared to the fourth through seventh chakras – the Heart chakra through the Crown chakra – which are considered to be in the realm of the spiritual.

Meditation, and more specifically, your personal practice of meditation, will allow you to evolve into the higher spiritual realm, which is already an integral part of who you are.

Having a Seat at the Table Meditation

One other practice that is very powerful when you want to find answers to the questions that are particularly difficult to answer, is to do the 'Having a Seat at the Table' meditation. This will get you in touch with hidden aspects of yourself and breakdown the walls and blockages you've built that keeps you from seeing clearly and accessing your own internal wisdom.

For this meditation, first quiet the mind as you would for any of the meditative exercises discussed earlier.

Next, visually create your own special room inside of a special building, house, or cottage. This created space will be your sacred place to return to get answers anytime you choose. Creating a room is better than an outside space for this meditation because it allows you to focus more keenly on the task at hand.

You will be envisioning everything from the street that leads to your building to the outside of the building itself (what it looks like, the building entrance, etc.) Also, visualize the path that follows to the room you will be utilizing and everything inside from the table, chairs, other room furnishings and floor coverings, as well as the size, shape, and ceiling height of the space.

See yourself walking on the street, entering the building and making your way to this special room. Whether you're taking an elevator or walking through a door, see yourself actively participating and picture every step. Now picture a beautiful, well-proportioned table that's to your liking, with the exact chairs you wish to have for the guests you will be inviting. See your table however you wish to place it in the room. Notice all the artwork, windows, doors, railings, area rugs, and other furnishings.

At this table, you will have as many guests as you wish to invite – I find from three to seven guests to be most beneficial. Your guests can be from any period of time, current or past, historically famous or from your personal relationships…anyone who you wish to have assist you as you search for the wisdom needed to answer your important question.

Each guest that you choose should exemplify some aspect of a possible solution (compassionate, intellectual, rational, creative, financial, or solution oriented, etc.) that you may be overlooking or having difficulty reaching.

Walk to the table and see the individuals you have chosen sitting at your table and welcome them. After a brief introduction as to why you have called them to be here, ask your question to each guest, and let the answers free-flow from your invited participants. Each guest will bring their own perspective and expertise to your decision making process, and many times it will be something that you were not able to identify or see previously.

You can also engage in a dialog with your participants, asking for further clarity when needed. The information that comes forth will broaden your understanding and give you perspectives that were previously unattainable to you because you blocked out this part of you for whatever reason. In this place of deeply connected meditation, you are in touch with the collective subconscious as well as opening up the deeper levels of your own psyche. Knowledge and wisdom will come to you in new, beneficial, and novel ways with just a small amount of practice.

From this connected state of consciousness, ask one or two of your questions. (During your next meditation, you can ask another.) Do I need to hold on to this or is it better to let it go? Who am I really and what path should I follow? What is my life's purpose and what am I supposed to accomplish in this lifetime for the betterment of all? What are the most important things in my life and am I honestly living in accord with these deepest values? What path should I take and what should be my next step? Should I break away from the norm and go after this opportunity? How do I best resolve my current issue (explain to your guests the events, issues, and people involved)?

I often times have Mother Theresa joining me and when I ask her what she thinks I am missing or what I should do given my current situation, I always get an answer that evokes compassion. Yes, we all have compassion, but sometimes it gets kicked to the curb and isn't as front and center as it should be. What type of answer would you expect from Mother Theresa other than one that evokes compassion? This opens my compassionate side and brings this information back into the decision-making process and I gain a broader understanding and view that may have eluded me previously.

I sometimes have Thomas Jefferson stop in. I always appreciate his intellectuality, insightfulness, and his ability to find compromise in difficult situations. Carl Jung and Joseph Campbell are two of my favorite authors and I have had them sit in to share their perspectives – and they usually expand my limited viewpoint quite effectively with deeper meaning. With this, I am not channeling any past souls but soliciting those qualities both in myself and in the collective unconscious, which often opens up my limited thinking about a situation.

You may want to invite Buddha, the stoic Marcus Aurelius, Dr. Martin Luther King, or a special grandparent – anyone whose strengths may be temporarily lacking in your immediate perspective – and you don't know what's lacking until you have it introduced to you by one of your guests. That's why surrounding yourself with a variety of different perspectives is most productive.

It is best to know and understand the philosophy of the person you invite, so you can glean the wisdom they have mastered. Read up on the guests you wish to invite to your meeting if you are not familiar with their wisdom. This will make a deeper source of knowledge available to you and add much needed insight.

You are the master of this meditation – it's your space, your room, and your table! These are also your questions, as you are the moderator. This allows you to uncover needed answers by reaching more broadly into your internal self, assisting you in finding the correct path forward.

You can come to this place anytime you want. Just decide on your question and your personally selected invitees, then go to your Spiritual Center and once there, visualize the room you've previously created.

When you ask your question to each of your guests, unbiased perspectives will be expanded and your path forward will be made clear. It's you and you alone that must make the journey to healing and self-realization.

> *"If you are not willing to risk the unusual, you will have to settle for the ordinary."*
>
> ~ Jim Rohn

In You Must Go!

In Star Wars, Yoda (talking about the Dagobah Tree Cave) tells Luke: "That place… is strong with the dark side of the Force. A domain of evil it is. In you must go." When Luke asks what is in the cave, Yoda responds: "Only what you take with you." When Luke starts to grab his physical weapons, Yoda tells him: "Your weapons… you will not need them."

The cave is an age-old mythological symbol representing what lies beneath the surface and is to the individual, a frightening place of unexplored geography, fraught with danger – especially because of the unknown entities that must be faced and conquered.

In many ancient cultures the passage from boyhood to manhood was initiated by the adult men of the village placing an artifact deep, deep, inside a dark and dangerous cave. Now the boy beginning his initiation journey had to face and overcome his fears by going into the unknown cave in complete darkness and retrieve the object completely on his own with no outside assistance. Only when he returned with the object could it known that he had left the safety of his world, met, dealt with, and overcame his fear. This is the act of leaving his boyhood and entering into his manhood. It is also the act of letting go of one reality and evolving into what he was meant to become in life, in this case, a full-fledged adult who has met and overcame his fear.

When Yoda directs Luke to lift his X-wing fighter out of the muddy swamp, Luke responds by saying: "All right, I'll give it a try." Yoda harps on Luke: "No! Try not. Do. Or do not. There is no try." After Luke's attempts fail, he says: "I can't. It's (the task) too big." Yoda tells him: "Size matters not" and then shows Luke it can be done by lifting the X-wing fighter out from being stuck in the deep mud of the swamp and sets it down gently onto the beach. Luke exclaims: "I don't... I don't believe it!" Yoda says: "That is why you fail."

What is in the cave that *you* must enter? What is it that you must face? It's different for everyone. Each journey is comprised of an amalgamation of all of your life's experience. Everyone processes things differently and the only uniting thing that I can see is that we all process a lot of it incorrectly. This results in the storage of beliefs that can often shape our lives in detrimental ways.

This is what holds us back from achieving our self-realization and our life's purpose. Many will find excuses for not going into the cave, but *in you must go*, if you want to realize the life that you were meant to live.

We are moved and awakened when we see the pain in others; yet so often we turn and look the other way when we have the chance to see the pain in ourselves. If you find and use the innate powers you have within you, you can direct yourself to the path you are supposed to be on, which will bring you to self-realization and the fulfillment of *your own* life's potential.

The place that this work needs to be done is in your Spiritual Center. Go there, identify your Dragons, slay them, and re-recreate the world you wish to live in...the choice, and the journey, *is* yours to take.

> "You must have chaos within you to give birth to a dancing star."
>
> ~ Friedrich Nietzche

> "Science is organized knowledge. Wisdom is organized life."
>
> ~ Emanuel Kant

Reflecting on this chapter, I invite you to write down any applicable thoughts, take-aways, or lightbulb moments that your inner-self is realizing and trying to communicate to you:

_____

_____

_____

_____

_____

_____

_____

_____

_____

_____

Growing Your Awareness, Understanding, and Wakefulness

The Quantum Truth

When you look at everything in the universe, it all consists of the same stuff, just in different arrangements. Almost 99% of the human body is made up of just six elements that are found all over the universe: oxygen, carbon, hydrogen, nitrogen, calcium, and phosphorus.

All matter is energy and energy, in all of its various forms, permeates the entire universe. You can see a solid piece of wood release its stored energy by just putting a match to it or tossing it on a fire. This stored energy would be released in the form of heat and light energy. If you get around to splitting atoms (Solid matter? No, stored energy!) you obviously can release a tremendous amount of energy.

This omnipresent energy is, by definition, everywhere in the universe as explained by science. Religions talk about the particular God they designed as the source of what everything came from and to which everything will turn back into, and this energy source permeates everything in existence. Notice any similarities?

This omnipresent energy can be described as Universal Energy, Spirit, Source, God, the Soul, or you may just call it Life itself. My point is that if we and the universe are all made from the same stuff, then "I" and the "universe" are the same and vice versa, albeit in slightly different groupings!

I have a mantra based on this, and when I have reached my Spiritual Center through the practice of meditation, I repeat this mantra to myself: "I and the universe are the same. I am you; you are me – everyone and everything is the same and we are all connected together. I am in All, and All is in me. Show me the path that I should be on, and I will show you I have the courage to follow it."

Every atom and every subatomic particle is energy, and it doesn't matter if it is in a rock or a tree or a human – it's all energy. In Quantum Physics, at the subatomic level, matter and energy constantly change into each other – back and forth from energy to matter and matter to energy, over and over again. Particle physicists commonly measure the mass of a particle as units of energy.

We all know mass is energy and energy is mass from Albert Einstein's famous equation $E=MC^2$ (energy = mass times the speed of light squared). Therefore, the mass of your body is energy (and you could make the argument, so is your spirit because everything is energy). Knowing that you are energy, and everything is energy, allows you the possibility to connect on an energetic level with everyone and everything, anytime, and anywhere.

One last thing on Quantum Physics that I find interesting is that of entanglement, which states a particle can be in two places at the same time – even on the other side of the universe – and still be energetically connected. What happens to one particle will be instantaneously communicated to the other, and it is the Observer that manifests the particle into reality by their observance. The other particle vanishes at the very moment the chosen particle manifests by observance into reality.

This has turned classical physics on its head and may sound crazy and hard to comprehend, well, because, no doubt, it certainly is. But splitting atoms seemed at one point to be so impossible that no one could even conceive of the idea.

It's Life itself that keeps moving forward and will continue to do so. If mankind were to go extinct, Life in the universe would continue to evolve just fine. It's this energy that is ubiquitous and omnipresent, and the source of all creation. (Man does not weave the web of life. He is merely a strand in it – Chief Seattle). It is what we and all possibilities are made of.

Let's use another analogy to explain entanglement that is easier to understand: Let's say you are at a proverbial 'fork in the road' and you have to choose between two different possibilities. At this time both possibilities really do exist in reality – you can choose either choice as you see fit – but they only exist as "potentialities". The two choices both have an equal chance of being manifested in reality. Once you, the Observer, choose which choice you want to manifest into reality, the other choice is annihilated and disappears in time. This second potentiality never manifested in your life or in reality…just like the subatomic particle that is in two places but still connected energetically.

If I was choosing to go to a restaurant last week on Friday night, and I had it down to two of my favorite places, both choices existed as a potentialities. I happened to choose the second restaurant on my list, because I hadn't been there for a while. Going to the first restaurant on my list at the same exact time, last Friday night, never made it into reality as the event never happened, even though it did exist in reality as a potentiality (and that potentiality is now gone forever!) Once I (the Observer) made my choice, the other potentiality vanished, just like particles do in the Quantum Realm. I will never be able to go back in time and go to the first restaurant on my list last Friday night. I manifested my reality out of the possibilities I had (or potentialities).

Now think about how everything (and I mean *everything*) is made up of atoms, which are made of subatomic particles, and that everything is energetically connected, and you can begin to understand the interconnectedness of the "All". It really is at the forefront of science, as well as the teachings of ancient sages throughout history. Cool stuff to talk about, but much cooler to experience for yourself.

The first step to manifesting the future you desire is to understand who you really are and how you are connected to everything. Practicing being connected to the "All" through meditation will get you to your inner self – your Spiritual Center – and this is, your connection to everything.

> *"We have not even to risk the adventure alone.*
> *For the heroes of all time have gone before us.*
> *The labyrinth is thoroughly known,*
> *we have only to follow the thread of the hero path.*
> *And where we had thought to find an abomination,*
> *we shall find a god.*
> *Where we had thought to slay another,*
> *we shall slay ourselves.*
> *Where we had thought to travel outward,*
> *we shall come to the center of our own existence.*
> *And where we had thought to be alone,*
> *we shall be with all the world."*
>
> ~ Joseph Campbell,
> The Hero with a Thousand Faces

Self-Talk and Manifesting Outcomes

What you 'think' about determines how you feel. How you 'feel' will determine what you do, and what you 'do' determines the outcomes that you manifest.

You *can* actively control your thoughts through self-talk. What you tell yourself repeatedly every day will have an impact on your self-programming as it reinforces or breaks down your internal picture. This will have a very positive or a very detrimental effect on what you continually manifest in your life.

Structure your own self-talk to be a positive affirmation. If you say, "I'm glad I'm not affected by a financial struggle anymore." What image do you conjure up and imprint in your mind? A financial struggle! Rather, say to yourself, "I'm glad I am now living with financial abundance, and all my needs are comfortably met." This reinforces your internal picture, projects clarity, and increases your empowerment and strength.

The negative side of self-talk is both destructive and stealthy. Most of us don't realize what we tell ourselves repeatedly throughout the day – every day! You probably know someone (hopefully this isn't you) that always says: "Why do bad things always happen to me?" and sure enough, they manifest bad things on a consistent basis. If you call a friend or family member and say, "Oh, it's just me." What do you mean *it's Just You*! You should be saying this is the most wonderful, beautiful, and happy person in the world, and aren't you lucky because I'm calling you! We are all responsible for the self-image we create, as well as its upkeep and maintenance.

You can dismiss and reject whatever falsehoods from earlier programming that you know are not serving you well by controlling your self-talk, and therefore your internal picture. You can embrace and accentuate the beneficial thoughts that will cause you to take the actions necessary to bring about any life that you can imagine. The vast majority of people who fulfill their dreams are not any different from you, except for how they think and see themselves in their internal picture. This is what motivates them to take the actions that create the results they consistently achieve.

In *Think and Grow Rich*, which was written in 1937, Napoleon Hill explains how thoughts are things. If you have any doubts that thoughts have the power to create things, just think of everything you see around you, and realize it was first a thought before it was manifested into our world. The only possible exception would be if something was made accidentally while attempting to make something else, but even then, once realizing the new potential, you have thought bringing the new product or service to market.

Another way to look at how thoughts can manifest things and

events into reality is by the following example, which you should be able to relate to: Let's say you are watching a scary Halloween horror film and you hear some kind of noise outside your home. In reality it could be the neighbor's dog or a raccoon, or just the wind blowing on a branch that is now tapping on the side of your house – but you know the real cause – you just know there is an evil character out there, very similar to the character in the horror movie, and he is figuring out a way to quietly break in and do to you what has just been done in the horror film. So what happens? Your blood pressure raises quickly, your fight or flight response kicks in, and your adrenalin goes through the roof! All because of a thought, and it doesn't even need to be an accurate thought, yet you definitely manifest all kinds of physical things into reality that can be measured with the appropriate measuring equipment!

There is no doubt that thoughts can actually manifest things and events into reality. You could also think about the placebo effect… how do you think that works? It all rests in the power of thought to create reality!

Another example is to imagine right now that you are in your kitchen and holding a perfectly ripe, nice bright yellow and extremely juicy lemon – picture this in your mind. Now cut the lemon in half and feel the juice run all over your fingers. See yourself lifting one half of the cut lemon up to your tongue, and slide your tongue all over the lemon – feel it on your tongue and taste the lemon juice as you squeeze the lemon to release a flow of lemon juice that runs into and completely fills your mouth.

Did just the thought of this make you salivate? Thoughts are deeply powerful and shape our physical, mental, and emotional health on a daily basis. This is not only on frivolous things, but also on major life-changing things.

Make sure that your thoughts and your self-talk reinforce the outcome you are looking to achieve. Be creative with them and use them to your advantage. Consistency and repetitiveness is the key.

The Old Self-Talk	The New Self-Talk
I don't see how I could do that.	I will figure out a way and it will be fun!
Hmm. That will never happen.	I will keep learning and improving until I make it happen!
Hey, it's just me.	Hey, it's me!
It seems like I'll never do it.	It's my world and I will manifest what I want, and discard what is not the right path. I create what's in my life – no one else does! This is what I am going to create, and no one can stop me!

Lastly, you have to realize that the way to accomplish everything already exists. We may not know how to get it done at the current moment, but that doesn't mean that the way doesn't exist. It's just waiting to be figured out.

If you talked about landing a man on the moon or splitting an atom, one hundred years before these things were accomplished, there is a good chance you would have been considered a lunatic and locked up. When these things were accomplished it was because the way to do it (which existed from the beginning of time) had finally been discovered.

For a long time no one thought a human being could run a four-minute mile. The predominant thought was that the heart would explode or some other physical tragedy would result from trying to accomplish this. On May 6, 1954, Roger Bannister was the first person to run a one-mile distance in less than four minutes. Since his groundbreaking performance, 1,497 other athletes have now broken this record. What once seemed impossible becomes possible, if we believe it is possible. It just takes some work and a change in how we see the world.

> *"All truth passes through three stages. First, it is ridiculed. Second, it is violently opposed. Third, it is accepted as being self-evident."*
>
> ~ Arthur Shopenhauer

> *"Discovery consists of seeing what everybody has seen and thinking what nobody else has thought."*
>
> ~ Albert Szent Gyorgy

Internal/External Picture

Your Internal Picture is your personal belief system about yourself. We form our belief system from input we accept from others, with the majority of it coming before adulthood. We take this information, twist it around, and then look for confirmation that our judgements are correct. This confirmation can come from other sources of incorrect information, or from the same improper sources that originated our inaccurate views. This internal picture forms the foundation of our self-worth and creates our self-judgements that determine how we see and understand our place in the world.

Self-talk, which are the things we continually tell ourselves, reinforces this internal picture that we have already formed. This reinforcement strengthens and engrains this picture we hold on to so tightly and we tend to accept this as truth because we don't have an alternative picture to compare it to.

The feedback loop that we live with starts with the external input from others who we assigned some degree of authority. As mentioned before, this could be our parents, aunts, uncles, our third grade teacher, or other prominent or influential people during our childhood years. The things we rightfully or wrongfully accept as true are then reinforced by other events later in our lives. Once we accept this initial picture as true, we look for ways to validate what we've come to believe about ourselves, and tell ourselves that this is both accurate and true. Therefore, our Internal Picture creates and feeds our self-talk, and then our self-talk reinforces what we've chosen to hold as our Internal Picture and our feedback loop is set in place.

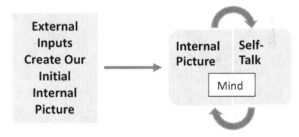

One of the most important ways to change our Internal Picture is to change our self-talk. This breaks the reinforcing and repetitive input cycle. When this cycle is interrupted, a need for congruency is created.

It's your Internal Picture that creates the self-sabotage that makes you quit while you are advancing in order to keep your reality matched up with the way you currently see yourself. This is what limits all of us! If you want to manifest something different from what you currently have, changing your Internal Picture is crucial.

Let me share with you a real life example that happened to me at work, and this had perplexed me for years: A number of years ago I was doing sales training for a large company. I could consistently improve sales performance with some of the salespeople who were struggling, and they would see a tripling in their sales performance consistently within days of their training. I did this with many people, but they all shared the same outcome in the end. After proving to every one of their coworkers that they could perform at this advanced level, totally on their own without any outside help, they all reverted back to their old, past, sub-par performance levels, usually after eight to ten weeks of success. I tried and tried to figure out why they wouldn't stay with three-times the paycheck plus tons of accolades – it just seems to me like everyone would. However, time and time again the same eventual failure happened, and, when asked, none of them had a good answer.

About two years after I stopped my sales training someone told me about our internal and external picture and everything became clear to me. If our Internal Picture says we can't do something, or we're not worthy or deserving of reaching a higher degree of success, then it doesn't matter even if we prove to ourselves that we can, because it's the stronger vision inside of us that dominates and directs our lives. If our Internal Picture says we can't achieve something or are not worthy of having something, we will do whatever it takes to make reality match up to this. Our Internal Picture is always the most powerful driver of our behavior and if we are not in accord with it, we feel like we are living a lie.

If you were always told you couldn't do something or you weren't worthy of having something, this will most likely be your current reality. This feedback loop causes you to repeat the same old patterns. This is what has produced your past and current results. By changing your own self-talk and altering your internal picture, you will create a future that is of your own design, and will likely look dramatically different from your past. Einstein's definition of insanity was repeating the same thing over and over again and expecting a different result.

Even if you prove to yourself that you can accomplish something, you will likely revert back to that engrained and entrenched reality even if it's not in your best interest and you've already proven to yourself you are fully capable of creating something better. It's like having an internal thermostat that you set a temperature range for your comfort zone. If you exceed the upper level you have set, you'll sabotage any current or further gains to get you back to the level where you think you belong. If you fall below the lowest level of your comfort zone, you'll step it up to get back to the level that you *think* is your proper place. All of these levels that we set are completely arbitrary.

Our external picture is how we purposely portray ourselves to the outside world and it is how the world actually sees us. This can be quite different from our internal picture.

So what do your internal and external pictures look like? Look seriously at how your life is now, and this will give you a good indication of what you hold as your internal and external pictures. You will see the settings you have (arbitrarily) chosen for your thermostat. Do you find success easily? Have you already obtained the life you want; are you well on your way to achieving that life? Do you find your relationships are better than you could have ever imagined?

When our internal and external pictures are not in accord, we experience internal conflict. We all have a strong and natural tendency to move toward conflict resolution...so the stronger of these two pictures will dictate what we do and determine what we have as far as the current situations in our lives.

The way to change our internal picture is to become cognizant of what it is and then decide what we want our new picture to be. The stronger, more ingrained old picture we hold has been with us for years or even decades, reinforced over and over millions of times by our own daily self-talk and will not want to be replaced. It will be stubborn and keep coming back saying you can't reach this new level, why are you even trying? When this happens, just say with conviction, "No! That used to be me, but that's not me anymore! Now I am this way! This is who I am now!" This is how our self-talk interrupts the repetitive pattern of our old internal picture, eventually dislodging it, making it possible for our new, more beneficial, internal picture to be inserted and become dominant.

Another thing that's helpful is to think about how bad you will feel if you don't take control and create the life you want to have...

who will you have let down? Think also, about how wonderful you will feel when you reach the success you want to create! What will that feel like when you look around and know that you actually accomplished the dream that you are now only thinking about? How good will that feel?

Tying our emotions to our desires is a powerful tool and we can use both the desirable outcomes and the undesirable consequences of not taking action to propel us to where we want to go. Becoming emotionally invested and staying steadfast on our new path are extremely necessary to accomplish the outcomes we wish to manifest.

As we give concerted and sustained effort to the new and more desirable picture through self-talk, visualization, and meditation, our new Internal Picture gains strength and the old picture fades away. This is finding, facing, and slaying your Dragons, which is needed in order to move forward and break the grip of the old limiting internal vision that we hold of ourselves.

We also need to envision how our new life is going to be. We need to see, hear, and feel the new currently less dominant picture that we want to create, and really live it now – continuously! You really should see yourself in your newly created life; hear others conversing with you like you have already developed yourself and have already arrived in the future; and feel your emotions carry yourself right into the future "you" – feel what it will be like when you are actually living what you are now creating!

Depak Chopra, in his creation *The Way of the Wizard* explains that most people say, "When I have that, then I'll do that, then I'll be that. And they find this is very limiting. But the Wizard [the evolved you] reverses that and says: I'll be that, then I'll do that, and then I'll have that. And life becomes much more enjoyable...That's when the miracles start to happen."

What you are about to do is take control over the direction of your life. By changing the barrage of information that comes to all of us a million times a day. We can truly create a life full of accomplishment and joy.

If you question how powerful this technique is, try counting how much time you spend thinking...how many thoughts do you have in one hour? Experts from Queen's University in Canada, say the average mind will have about 6,200 thoughts per day. Then multiply this by 365 days per year. How many of these thoughts have been reinforcing your old belief system (founded or unfounded)? And this is only one year of reinforcement; how many years of reinforcement do you have working for or against you? (We haven't even talked about how many dreams you have in a year and their influence or meanings yet!)

You can see the preprogramed barrage of information that influences us constantly, often times even subliminally, and this may seem beyond our control, but it's really not!

Here's another quick example of how powerful and necessary it is to make the new picture congruent with what you want to manifest if you want to bring about change into your life: I had just moved to the other side of Denver and had stopped into a new hair salon to get a haircut. The woman cutting my hair started with the usual small talk, and then asked me if I smoked. Being vegan for many years and priding myself on a healthy lifestyle, I replied with a quick – No! Then I thought it must have been some sort of a rhetorical question, so I asked her if she did. She told me she was trying to quit and hadn't smoked in fourteen days, and that her last record was twenty one days and she would like to at least beat that, and hopefully quit forever. I replied that I didn't think she had any chance at all of making it. She looked at me aghast!

I smiled and asked her what do smokers who are trying to quit do? After some delay and no answer, I answered: "They always start smoking again because they see themselves (internal picture) as smokers." Then I asked her "What do non-smokers do?" and she replied, "Well, they don't smoke." I replied, "Yes, that's right, because they see themselves as non-smokers!"

I then told her as soon as she changes her internal picture and sees herself as a non-smoker she'll never pick up a cigarette again, because that's what non-smokers do – they never touch another cigarette because they find it to be massively gross and repulsive. But if your internal picture tells you that you are a smoker, you don't even really have a chance – you're just going to stay addicted.

It seemed like a lightbulb went off in her head, and I hope our exchange helped her understand what she was up against. Who we are and what we accomplish is all about what our internal picture is. You have to first *see* the future and *be* the future you want in order to manifest it.

In time, the new picture will become stronger and stronger with your additional reinforcement, and nothing breeds success like success. Once you see the changes you've created, you will continue to grow, learn, and build. You will then become the new person you previously only wished to become.

It does take time and it does take effort, but it is a small price to pay when compared to the benefit of having the rest of your life enriched by self-realization, self-accomplishment, and self-fulfillment. Once you learn how to go to the center of your being and broadcast your intentions, uninhibited by the old Dragons that created your detrimental internal picture, your ability to create and manifest will be practically unlimited.

You will reach a point when you look around and realize you have made it, and accomplished everything you set out to do. Now determine what else you would like to accomplish. There is really nothing stopping you from creating more of what you want – the sky is pretty much the limit!

No one has the right to control or direct your life, or the life of any other person. We all have the right to self-realization and fulfillment. It is up to us, and only us, to become the person that we were destined to be.

> *There is nothing noble about being superior to another. The true nobility is in being superior to your previous self.*
>
> – Hindu Proverb

Audio, Visual, and Kinesthetic

We all need to communicate. There is no quality of life without love and communication.

I was at a wine tasting party over a Christmas holiday some years ago and as the crowd splintered off into smaller groups, we had in our group one woman who was a marriage counselor. You can probably guess the type of conversation that ensued. Early in this new conversation, one of the guests asked her what was the most common problem she would see in her line of work. Before having time to answer, someone jumped in and said that it had to be communication. She answered that communication was never a problem because, "we are always communicating". "Now it might be (F.U.) and that might be the problem, but we are always communicating something." I never forgot that.

If our response is no response at all or a delayed response, isn't that communicating? The tone of our voice, body gestures…that look – you know what that means!

I think good communication starts with understanding how we, as individuals, have our own unique way of communicating. If we don't understand the other person's style of communicating, we put ourselves in a position where it is difficult to best understand what is trying to be communicated and generally miss what is important to the other person. Have you ever thought that what you're communicating should just be plain obvious, and yet it seems the other person doesn't get it and doesn't seem to even have a clue? I'm sure you know the reverse is also true, and if you think not, just ask your partner. Different communication styles are likely the cause.

Psychology suggests there are three main learning modalities: Audio, Visual, and Kinesthetic. We use all of these at different times based on the particular task at hand. If attending a weekend painting class, we should be using our visual skills as we try to follow the instructor; when relaxing to or listening to new music, we will be using our audio abilities; and when we are showing compassion or consoling a friend in distress we engage our kinesthetic capabilities.

When we communicate with others, we all tend to have a dominate style that we use to automatically express ourselves, and likely a secondary style which would not be as dominant. This is easy to see once you know what to look for.

A person who is primarily an Audio communicator will use audio terms to describe what they want to communicate. They'll often say things like: "Do you *hear* me?" "That *sounds* good." "Have you *heard* the latest?" "If you listen closely, you can *hear* it." "*Talk* to me." and "I *hear* you." If you know someone who communicates this way you should definitely talk with them using the same type of audio vocabulary. Not that the other modalities should be ignored, but communicate in the receiving person's most dominant giving-and-receiving modality for the most effective communication.

If a person is primarily a Visual communicator, they will say things like: "I *see* what you're saying." (Even though it is impossible to *see* the sound waves that are being projected from your mouth.) "How's that *look* to you?" "Well, let's take a *look* at it." "Yeah, *show* me." "Let's *see* what you got." and "I'll believe it when I *see* it."

A person who is primarily a kinesthetic communicator is all about touching and feeling, and will be the first to dish out hugs or handshakes. They are also about feelings, like 'gut feelings' and tend to be more intuitive than most. They can pick up on subtle vibes better than most people do because of their increased ability to feel, and having a tactile response to their world is a given. They will use language that will expose their style of communicating by saying things like: "So, how do you *feel* about that?" "Oh, this *feels* so good!" "I don't have a good *feeling* about this." and "I know how you *feel*." You'll see them giving pats on the back to coworkers and nearly everyone they meet, every chance they get.

We also communicate love best in our preferred modality. In relationships, if you tend to express yourself with audio, you really appreciate it when a special someone tells you they love you, or says something sweet, compliments you, or maybe whispers sweet things in your ear.

A person who favors visual communication doesn't care about that hardly at all, because, after all, they are just words and words are cheap! Actions always speak louder than words – so show me! "Buy me some flowers, do something nice for me, or take me out to dinner and a movie...just *show* me!"

A person who expresses themselves kinesthetically will love holding their partner's hand in public and be more physically affectionate whenever the opportunity becomes available. Snuggling on the couch, watching a movie with their partner – what could possibly be better than that? They'll also be drawn to the tactile effect of clothing, furniture, etc. You will notice them being more empathetic and intuitive. They will communicate their affection from a place of caring and definitely from the heart. To them the world is all about feeling on every level.

Why is this important? Because we all communicate and receive love best when it is expressed in in the same way as our primary preference of expression. We will have the ability to understand the other modalities, but not as well or as efficiently as the main modality that we identify with personally.

I was in a relationship once with a visual communicator, and I'm a kinesthetic. I remember when she bought me a really expensive Waterman pen – like $100.00 for a pen! She said she just thought I should have a nice pen (she was *showing* me her love). I said thanks and gave her a hug (as a typical kinesthetic would do) but really thought my $10.00 pen worked just fine and looked good compared to the lower-priced $5.00 pens out there. I also had the habit of holding her more than she was accustomed to, and one day she exclaimed, "Why are you always touching me!" Neither one of us understood that we were communicating love in our own unique way, nor did we understand when the other person was communicating love in their unique way. Neither of us realized what was happening, or when it was happening. We were like the two ships passing in the night, and consequently the relationship didn't last all that long. Later, when I learned about the audio/visual/kinesthetic preferences, everything became clear to me. I learned to receive and communicate love in a much better way, and this improved my relationships tremendously.

We all have a primary preference for expressing ourselves, and we also have a secondary. Beth and I are both kinesthetic (Wahoo!!!) and as a secondary, I am an audio and Beth is a visual. It is important to learn each other's primary and secondary modality for communicating and loving and to discuss this with each other if you're in a relationship. You will notice the quality and effectiveness of your communications blossom. And remember – we're always communicating something.

> *"Well-being is a constant while happiness is a "thing."*
> – Martin Seligman

Dream Analysis

Dreams are an exciting way to become aware of the unknown ideas and concepts that are in your unconscious as well as your subconscious mind and unlock the treasure-trove of information and guidance that resides there. What resides in your subconscious mind are the things you are not fully aware of, but still have an influence on the actions you take. What resides in your unconscious is for the most part inaccessible to the conscious mind, but still effects your behavior and well-being. The information in dreams can come from either place. Your task is to decode these, or learn to decode these, so that this information becomes available to you.

The information stored in our subconscious can keep us limited and locked in place, or it can promote our growth and enhance our way forward. It is normally influenced or created by the events that shaped our early childhood, but is often times reinforced repeatedly by the perceptions of events later in life. This can have a profound impact on our current viewpoints.

A few possible examples could be something traumatic that your conscious mind delivered to your unconscious and now it seems to be stuck there forever. It could also be something not so traumatic that you were told repeatedly or saw repeatedly, and now you just do that without thinking about it – "It's just the way I was raised!"... "That's just ME!" "I don't know why I keep doing this same thing over and over!" Are these thought patterns currently serving you well? Are they something you want to keep, discard, or change?

Think of the unconscious mind as the lower part of the iceberg. It is not easily seen, but certainly is the driver of where the 'seen' part of the iceberg is going. This is why it is important to understand what is stored here – so we can sort through and discard what is no longer serving us and empower the images and concepts that will drive and properly direct the course of our lives.

Once you begin a serious quest for spiritual awakening, or start searching for important answers, your dreams will likely increase in number and significance. This will make new information available to you that will spawn new self-realizations. It's like: "Ask, and you shall receive."

Understanding the meanings, symbols, and events in a dream is completely unique to the dreamer. It is the dreamer's interpretation that is to be accepted, not the outside interpreter deciding what a symbol means for the dreamer by inserting his or her own personal biases. It is not possible to say if you dream of a certain event that it means this or that, it is totally dependent on what this experience means to the person having the dream.

An important first point is to understand that the conscious and the unconscious exchange information on a fairly regular basis. The communication lines between the two are like a two-way street. Your unconscious mind definitely feeds and exerts its influence into your conscious mind and your conscious mind definitely feeds and exerts its experiences into your unconscious mind.

The thoughts and ideas that come from the unconscious to the conscious can be divided into two categories. First, is the Personal Unconscious which was groomed by the personal experience of the individual. Second, is the Collective Unconscious, which is the result of eons of repetitive experiences garnered by the vast majority of individuals belonging to the human race, and this collective experience is definitely passed on. Out of our personal unconscious come various complexes; out of our collective unconscious come the archetypical images that all of mankind share and share alike.

The Collective Unconscious may prove to cast an even wider net than that, possibly reaching into the Gaia principle, first put forth in the 1970s by the chemist James Lovelock and co-developed by the microbiologist Lynn Margulis, which states the idea that all living things on earth may be part of one large single organism – Mother Earth! At the very least, each one of us has the whole of humanity as an integral part of our own psyche, undoubtedly. Think of the sages of old that stated we are one with everything.

Mythological symbols that are incorporated into the Collective Subconscious are ubiquitous and permeate our modern societies. We can see them in most movies, childhood stories, as well as societal practices. If we just look, we will see them everywhere.

A few common archetypical images that are recognized in mythology, as well as dreams, are: the father/mother figure, the unknown helper, the wise old man, the virgin birth (which is a spiritual birth, not a physical birth), the Creator/the Destroyer/the giver of life, the Healer, the Hero, the Jester, the Caregiver, the Rebel, the Seeker, and the animals that show us the magical way and bestow untold wisdom upon us. These images have the opportunity to transform us for the better if we are able to gain from the knowledge they offer and represent.

These primordial concepts, found in practically all mythologies and cultures from all over the world, are from as far back in time as we can trace. All the major religions incorporate these and call them their own, but if you take a wider look, they're present everywhere because they are embedded deep in the human psyche!

Here are some basic explanations of other shared symbols – to be taken with a grain of salt and adjusted to individual circumstances. Most of these symbols are also universal, meaning everyone around the world has similar experiences and expressions, such as being under water, physically flying, falling, or being chased. They can also be interpreted as individualized and personal, relating to specific events in your life.

If you dream you are in water or coming out of water, this is generally understood to mean that this information is coming from your unconscious realm so pay attention – this is a hugely important matter!

If you dream of someone in your dream that you do not know, they are likely to represent a different aspect of your own personality. This is really another partial version of yourself.

If we can't understand the symbols of a particular dream, it doesn't mean they're of no value, it only means we are incapable of understanding them at this time.

I had a conversation with a woman who explained to me a dream that she recently had. In her dream she was holding hands with a number of small children on both her right and left sides while under a very large amount of water (again, water generally indicates you are in the realm of the subconscious – so pay attention. This is likely to be important!) She mentioned that no one thought they would make it out alive and survive this terrible situation, but somehow they did. She also mentioned that when they finally started to come out of the water, they were fighting against very large ocean waves while making their way to shore. She – with all the children still on either side, hands clasped tightly together – saw a large number of dead fish all around them. At first she thought these dead fish were really gross, but then she quickly changed her perspective (transformative), and saw that the dead fish were, in fact, a good source of food that was plentiful and bountiful, and easily available as nourishment for herself and the children.

I offered up a quick interpretation that being completely submerged in water and then coming out of it usually indicates this information is something deep in the subconscious that wants to, or needs to, come into the conscious realm. All of the children holding on tightly together were likely different facets of her fractured or splintered inner child. Self-realization and healing is really all about the integration of the various facets of ourselves so that we can become one whole, integrated, healthy adult, and move on and become what we are meant to be.

The large amount of abundant food (fish) that was all around her was letting her know not to worry, that all the nourishment (love and support) she needs "*is*" all around her and easily available. Her subconscious mind is offering up this information to her conscious mind to let her know that even though she had a difficult childhood, she made it through the difficult times and is now surrounded by all the abundance she needs to live a happy and healthy life. In short: relax, you've made it, let the past go, and now move into and enjoy your current and future life powered by the abundance of Love that surrounds you!

Wouldn't having this information coming from your subconscious give you a boost of confidence and allow you to move through the healing process and get to the better place you are longing for? She can and should look to the future with great anticipation rather than dwelling in a painful past. This is exactly what healing looks like – letting go of the grip that the past has on you, and embracing the abundance that is all around you, as well as looking forward to the bright future that is waiting to be created.

Your unconscious mind also picks up on things that are missed by your conscious mind in day-to-day activities, and these things can also be revealed in dreams, often in strange and weird ways, through the same use of personal and collective symbolism.

Why does the unconscious seem to sometimes mask its

communication and express the information in riddles? It seems that painful aspects will often times be disguised in an attempt to make the information available, but with a less damaging delivery – a sort of sugar-coating or euphemism, if you will.

While you are seeking on your own personal journey, you will likely find what treasures and haunts exist in your unconscious. Yes, there are Gods and Demons there, but ignoring them will only keep you from evolving into the higher and healthier place that is waiting for you.

Our personalities can be fragmented and include many different aspects. The information communicated from our dreams can offer glimpses of these different fragments and offer us ways to improve our lives by becoming more fully integrated.

Let's say you dream of a stranger who is a horrible person and very uncaring toward the other people in your dream. This may be showing you a hidden part of *your* psyche that you should look at. Could you be more compassionate or understanding? Your internal self, your unconscious, may be suggesting just that, and my guess is you would be far better off if you were to understand and incorporate this message into your conscious personality.

By making the unknown known, dreams can give you clarity and depth not obtainable in any other way. So let this natural process bring the hidden information from your subconscious and into your conscious.

Why do we all use symbols that are almost identical with only slight modifications to fit local circumstances, i.e., being chased by a white bear (landlocked) or a white whale (oceanic culture) even though in many cases there has been no contact or exchange of ideas between, say the Aborigines and the peoples of Iceland or of Eastern Europe? It's our connectedness that is expressed in our Collective Subconscious. We really are all connected.

A middle-aged woman, an acquaintance who was 36 years of age, came to me smiling and saying she just had the weirdest dream the night before. She *was* a baby giraffe with the cutest little stubby legs that made the giraffe look like it had the legs of a Bassett Hound. She mentioned it was as if the giraffe's legs were chopped off at the knees and then healed that way.

Now this giraffe was in a glass cube and wanted to go outside of the contained environment but couldn't because of the glass walls, ceiling and floor. Every time she (the giraffe) tried to join her other friends, she would hit the nearly invisible glass wall and this would prevent her from joining the outside world as she so desperately wanted. This was continually frustrating for her. She could see everyone and everything that was going on outside, but was unable to get there and be part of that life. I thought the symbology and expression from her unconscious was remarkable.

When she was thirteen years old she experienced the severe trauma of her mother committing suicide, and when seventeen, her father had a heart attack and died right in front of her. It seems, and understandably so, that the emotional scarring from the first tragedy left her psychologically frozen at the level of a thirteen-year-old person, unable to move on and develop into a fully functioning adult. The second trauma further solidified the stifling effect of the previous trauma, leaving her incapable of functioning properly in a normal society.

Although on the outside she was very pleasant, attractive, and definitely likeable, romantic relationships were never a part of her world. Her unconscious chose to liken the situation to a baby giraffe, who should be able to roam freely but instead, had been 'cut off at the knees' so to make normal movement crippling and almost impossible. Being in a glass cube (invisible walls that kept her locked in and unable to move on in life, as she should) represented something real but very difficult to see. You can also see her yearning to join the others (Life itself!) She was baffled as to the invisible barriers that were keeping her locked away and tormented in sort of an emotional prison. The information given, as I saw it, was that she needed to deal with the traumas that froze her emotional evolution so she could join the others and eliminate the isolation caused by these traumas still stored deeply in her unconscious. Although difficult, the resolution she should clearly take was well communicated by her own personal unconscious.

How many times have you had a dream that leaves you saying "Boy, that was weird!" and having no idea of the information being shared? The conscious and unconscious seem to speak to each other most often in a secret code, or at least it seems like that. You can think of each half of this dichotomy as being from a completely different realm, and therefore they speak in different languages. Just as two people speaking different languages on a street corner today can still get their ideas across by using sign language or gestures, albeit with some difficulty, the information and communication can still be harvested and utilized.

One helpful technique is to record a series of dreams in a dream journal as this can shed a better light on the information that is trying to come through. Have you ever read a paragraph and didn't understand a particular word, but by looking at the surrounding words you could understand its meaning? The same is true for information that is being conveyed to you through your dreams; this sheds a better light on things and makes the message more accessible. If you do not understand the message that is trying to come through, your unconscious will likely give you the same message in a slightly different way on different occasions, usually in the near future, until you understand what is being communicated.

Carl Jung speaks of the Anima and the Animus – the feminine and masculine part of our personality that both genders have in varying degrees, so every male has some degree of feminine qualities, and every female has some degree of masculine qualities. This is visually expressed in the yin/yang symbol so well known in the Asian cultures. In this symbol, the Yin (feminine) has a little bit of Yang in it and the Yang (masculine) has a little bit of Yin in it, and together they form the whole being. This is represented by a circle (the circle is another motif that shows up everywhere in the world and in all cultural mythologies).

Male and female individuals showing up in our dreams can represent these internal aspects of ourselves and point to potential areas that need attention.

Yin is feminine and is represented by the black area.

Yang is masculine and is represented by the white area.

Jung also speaks of the Shadow – the part of our unconscious that is not recognized by our conscious. Dreams and their symbols expose this information, and if properly understood, reveal much needed information that is crucial to our wholeness and our process of self-integration.

Changing or eliminating the unwanted facets may seem like an impossible task, but it's not. Going into your unconscious and discovering what things are stored there is the first –and most crucial – step to creating any amount of lasting change. It will give you the ability to redirect and take ownership in the creation of how you want the rest of your life to be.

Understanding psychology and mythology will increase your ability to understand symbolism and make far better use of the information that is coming from your unconscious. The information dreams can provide will give you strength, courage, and understanding, or further affirm a position you're considering. They can also express hidden information that needs to come into your conscious thoughts so you can better understand and act on current challenges. This will put you in a better position to know the best way to move forward.

Your Ego is your conscious mind, or the thoughts, memories, and emotions that react to the outside world as you see it. It's how you understand yourself to be – "I am this; I am that". The ego can be changed as new information is introduced, so really, you can become what you envision yourself being, by changing your informational input.

Understanding the communication coming from your unconscious mind through the analysis of your dreams will reveal what lies secretly within you, and increase your understanding of what concepts or perceptions might need to be changed or altered.

Going inside, finding and sorting through the information we find – keeping what we want and eliminating what is holding us back – will be immensely helpful in manifesting the life we want to live. Information stored in our unconscious is usually unknown, repressed, or neglected.

Repeatedly asking the same question before going to sleep will provoke your unconscious to answering your inquiry. The answer will come to you either in a dream, as thoughts when you first wake up, or during the day when you least expect it and weren't even thinking about it. It can also come from the daily interactions with others when something seemingly unrelated jumps out and you see the answer to your question delivered to you without anyone else even knowing it. When you practice questioning on a regular basis, the answers will flow more consistently and deeper understandings will emerge.

You may find it helpful to share your dreams with a trusted friend who you can discuss your dreams with and the possible interpretations, and listen to theirs as well.

It is not my intention to go into great depth here on dream interpretation, but rather to introduce you to the possibilities and intrigue you into further reading, learning, and practicing. Even a single book dedicated to the subject would only barely scratch the surface. Rather, I hope to convey the necessity and importance of self-inquiry, which is vital in any search for truth. Finding the truth is essential to all future development.

Self-discovery is a personal journey. Understanding what is in your subconscious and unconscious states, conveyed through your dreams is extremely valuable. Deciding what positive adjustments are to be made to your Internal Picture, learning to project your intentions from your Spiritual Center, and taking action to ensure your plans are successful, are all part of this journey. This is not a frivolous undertaking, but rather one of undeniable importance.

> *"The next message you need is always right where you are."*
>
> ~ Ram Dass

Running from Pain

So many of us are running from pain, but we don't have to. Rather, just give it up. It may exist in the circle you are currently in, but there are many, many circles all around you. You can either fix the circle you're in by fixing yourself first, then sharing your process of evolution with others, or you can make your way to any other circle of your choosing.

You may or may not see these other circles now, but even if you don't, that doesn't mean they're not there. Just focus on how you want your life to be and you will begin to see that you have the power to get to that place you are envisioning. The question is: what will you accept and what will you not accept? This is what determines what your circle will look like. What will you settle for and what won't you settle for? The answers to these questions will define the majority of your future life experiences.

You may find that by changing the things you deem necessary, everything else will fall in-line for the better. In extreme cases, you may need to leave almost everything you know, have, and trust, and maybe you have to leave everything without exception. It might be some combination of these varying degrees that will provide you with the best results.

If you go to your Spiritual Center, and ask the deepest, most connected part of yourself for the best course of action for you to take, you will find the right answer is within you. Once you find your answer, act on the decision that is in your best interest.

When you see the path to further growth and the life you want to have, you, and only you, can answer the question of whether or not this is what's in your best interest. If you decide that it is, then move forward and make your new life. I know you'll be glad you did. It's amazing how doors can open up for us when we are on our true path and how they always stay shut when we are not on our true path. There are many beautiful people in the world and taking your own spiritual journey has a tendency of bringing beautiful people into your life. Like attracts like.

Many people have left poverty, or a life full of abuse, and have created a wonderful life for themselves. They had to 'not accept' one way and create another way, moving to an entirely new circle. Some have given up everything they knew and owned, and went off to become a Buddhist monk and now are world-renowned and travel the planet as they please. We all have many options and everything is possible if we take the necessary steps to manifest what we desire.

We are all Spiritual Beings. Spiritual Beings have no need to stay in any particular circle that is not conducive to their own growth and well-being. Being stuck or enslaved is the work of the ego. The ego is the small container; the universe is the large container – they are connected, and transitioning from one to the other is just a matter of scale.

When you find your Universally Connected Self by going inside, you will be empowered. Which "self" do you want to expand and further develop, and which "self" do you want to let wither? It's very similar to our internal/external picture. What we continually visualize will come into our lives if we take the necessary steps to manifest it. What we decide we will not accept any longer will cease to be and fade into our past – if we take action and purposefully create the life we envision and desire.

The point here is that you do have the power to choose. And once you choose to go down a certain road, you will meet the people you need to meet and the world will open in a much more desirable way – it is, in fact, already waiting for you right now as a potentiality and the universe is waiting for you (the Observer) to choose.

When you learn the things you need to learn and take the steps you deem necessary for a better life, your wisdom, understanding, and experiences will blossom far beyond what you are capable of seeing now.

So trust the Universe. And what is the Universe? It's all the energy from the past, as well as all the energy currently in play, plus the totality of all the energy of future events that have yet to happen. All energy circulates. It changes forms and morphs, but never really disappears. This is the dance of life. This is what we are all taking part in. How could we have a more powerful teacher and guide than this energy? This power is what you are made of and you will develop greater understanding if you decide to take your own internal journey of self-discovery.

> *"Learn to love yourself first, instead of loving the idea of other people loving you."*
>
> ~ John Spence

Reflecting on this chapter, I invite you to write down any applicable thoughts, take-aways, or lightbulb moments that your inner-self is realizing and trying to communicate to you:

_____

_____

_____

_____

_____

_____

_____

_____

_____

_____

_____

Programming Corrections

Patterns We Create

Often times we try to compensate for our internal pain or discomfort in an attempt to ease our suffering. If we suffered from being dominated, we might try to dominate others. If we didn't have control when we were young, we may try to control everything in our sight, including people, schedules, and interactions. If we grew up in a negative environment, which resulted in a poor self-image, we may have a tendency to put down others so as to make ourselves feel temporarily adequate or superior, or we may become withdrawn, insecure and mistrust others. If we were in an abusive environment, we may tend to lash out at others for the smallest of things or be overly hurtful or abrasive.

You can always see if your current path is working for you or not working for you by simply taking an honest account of your current condition. How are things in your world? If everything in your world is absolutely perfect, then no reason to change a thing. If your current thought processes and your way of understanding the world are not delivering a completely happy life along with all that you wish to have, then now may be the right time to take a deeper look and really do something about it. When you deal with the root causes, the needed changes will come into your life.

Sometimes you do not realize how debilitating these patterns can be until they display themselves in a way that makes you feel like there must be more to life than this, and you realize you are not living your true self and your life could unravel at any moment. This is often due to your earlier trauma. Mythologically, this is the story of the Phoenix, who after purposefully being consumed by fire, rises from the ashes and is reborn anew, as well as transformed so as to live again.

This is a major realization, and one that should not be taken lightly. Taking a truthful account of where you are is the only way to begin this journey. Fooling yourself will do little for anyone. If you don't change your internal picture your situation will not improve. You can change jobs, buy a new house, get a new car, find a new relationship, etc., but you will still be taking the old *you* with *you* into the new situation. So if going "inward" is the direction best to travel, how do I get there?

> *"If you don't have the power to change yourself, then nothing around you will change."*
>
> ~ Anwar Sadat

Desiderata

Go placidly amid the noise and the haste, and remember what peace there may be in silence. As far as possible without surrender be on good terms with all persons. Speak your truth quietly and clearly; and listen to others, even to the dull and the ignorant, they too have their story. Avoid loud and aggressive persons, they are vexations to the spirit.

If you compare yourself with others, you may become vain or bitter; for always there will be greater and lesser persons than yourself. Enjoy your achievements as well as your plans. Keep interested in your own career, however humble; it is a real possession in the changing fortunes of time.

Exercise caution in your business affairs, for the world is full of trickery. But let not this blind you to what virtue there is; many persons strive for high ideals, and everywhere life is full of heroism. Be yourself. Especially do not feign affection. Neither be cynical about love; for in the face of all aridity and disenchantment it is as perennial as the grass. Take kindly the counsel of the years, gracefully surrendering the things of youth.

Nurture strength of spirit to shield you in sudden misfortune. But do not distress yourself with dark imaginings. Many fears are born of fatigue and loneliness. Beyond a wholesome discipline, be gentle with yourself. You are a child of the universe, no less than the trees and the stars; you have a right to be here. And whether or not it is clear to you, no doubt the universe is unfolding as it should.

Therefore, be at peace with God, whatever you conceive Him to be. And whatever your labors and aspirations in the noisy confusion of life, keep peace in your soul. With all its sham, drudgery and broken dreams, it is still a beautiful world. Be cheerful. Strive to be happy.

Max Ehrmann 1927

Finding Your Internal Dragons

What is a Dragon? A Dragon is the image we hold onto as part of our internal picture that holds us back from creating all that we were meant to be and to create. It is also what causes you to veer off the course that you would normally have chosen, often to march to someone else's tune, rather than your own. Dragons are usually created from incorrect information that was inputted into our subconscious. Many of these thoughts we accept as true, and leave them to fester in our subconscious until they seem to be set in stone. Most of these limiting concepts are not true, nor are their applications valid!

Dragons often times are a result of a single event, or a series of multiple events that caused you to define yourself in a different way, or as having inherent characteristics. From this image, you can understand yourself to be an overachiever, someone in the middle who will always stay mediocre, or an underachiever. You will then see yourself as worthy and looking forward to everything that will be coming your way, as not being good enough to achieve the life you would like to have, or not worthy of anything valuable and dreading the future to some extent, and wondering why life continuously throws you down.

Of course you can be anywhere on this scale, but the point is that we insert an image, and this image forms the foundation that we operate from, and this effects the vast majority of the outcomes that we experience throughout our lives, regardless of what we would like them to be.

We can eliminate the dragons that we hold in our internal picture only after discovering the root causes that implanted them in the first place. To do this, we need to go back to each initial cause and correct the improper meaning we linked to the event, now with proper understanding and from an adult's perspective.

A few questions to ask yourself are: Do you have any thoughts about yourself that have no practical use and have a tendency to create reoccurring difficulties? What beliefs do you hold that are blocking you from achieving the life you know you want to have? Do you have something you absolutely know that you want to do, but you are constantly telling yourself you can't do it for any number of reasons, or you just can't ever seem to make it happen?

Through meditative practice and other internal work, you can find and correct the root causes. Once you find what is holding you back – you've found a Dragon. This is what keeps you from realizing the life you have envisioned.

Do you want to move forward or is staying stuck an option you will accept or consider? Everything is up to you to create in the current moment, and this action or non-action will determine your future. The present moment now, was in fact, the future that you created in your past. Our current choices determine what our world will be in the future.

Our inner limiting fears and predispositions usually go unnoticed by the conscious mind, so the inner work of meditation and visualization are necessary. When you go "inside" by means of meditation, internal questioning, and soul-searching for answers, you will meet your Dragons and decide your destiny. Once met, you be able to release that locked and entrenched energy, and transform it into the type of beneficial energy that will keep manifesting and expanding throughout your life in the positive direction that you have chosen.

Joseph Campbell talks about the mythological European Dragon in his PBS production *The Power of Myth with Bill Moyers* and describes this Dragon as hording gold, treasures, and virgins in his lair, guarding and guarding and guarding his honored treasure. Even though he (or she) holds on to these things and protects them with the greatest of tenacity, he (or she) actually has no use for any of them and these treasures cannot be used for anything for which they were intended. The result is a life that is bound by limitations on all accounts.

What your dragon is, or what your dragons are, can be any number of things, as all of our paths, and the way we interpreted past events, are unique. Often we twist and turn the original information until it negatively solidifies in our internal picture and our Dragon is born.

Our perceptions and acceptance of the negative things we've been told, directly or indirectly, determines the dragons we keep inside. Factuality or truth has nothing to do with it; it's only our interpretation of these past events that matter!

Dragons can displace the happiness and contentment we should all be experiencing in life. We can invalidate our negative interpretation of past circumstances and not let these perceptions influence our current and future life. No past events should have mental or emotional control over us and do so, only if we give them power.

Once we recognize our potential to manifest what we want for ourselves in this world, the past control and influence others had, and have, is nullified. That's why the steps explained earlier on meditation and manifesting are so important. They will give you the strength and courage to face your dragons.

What keeps you down or holds you back? If your answer is "I don't know?" I'd ask you "What if you did know – what would that look like?" What would you do if you knew you could accomplish anything you wanted to achieve? Would you really let the thoughts of 'someone else' (I don't care who they are!) hold you back and determine your entire life's written and unwritten history?

A.H. Almaas said in his book *The Diamond Approach* "You can't fill an inside hole from an outside source." If this is applicable to you, attempts to have someone else make you happy, ease the discomfort or pain, or help you to become the self-realized person you were meant to be, will all eventually fail. Others can offer descriptions of the path you need to take if it is known to them, but it is you, and you alone that must make the journey and slay your own Dragons.

If you just can't seem to find the right loving relationship that will last and bring a lifetime of joy and happiness, it is likely to be your internal Dragons that are tripping you up time and time again. Some patterns will covertly and repeatedly increase isolation and loneliness, or continually create rejection, while other patterns bring all the surprises and joys a fulfilling life has to give.

Taking measure of your current life will tell you the truth of what Dragons you have created so far. It is your choice whether to have more of the same or to change it to something else. You are both the explorer and the creator if you choose to breathe life into these parts of you. And you get to choose what you discover and what you create.

The first step in taking control is eliminating the chaotic chatter that continually runs through your mind, as well as all of the societal programming and autonomic conditioning that constantly bombards you. This will allow you to come into contact with your Spiritual Center and you will really get to know who you are. When you operate from this place, you will be able to find your Dragons, deal with them, and create the destiny of your choosing. Beautiful Connected Innocence, altered by Dragons, puts most of us on our current trajectory.

You are likely aware of the stories where other individuals rose from poverty, broken or abusive homes, as well as other extreme hardships, and exalted themselves to live incredible lives, traveling the world at their pleasure, and being surrounded by an abundance of love and happiness. If they did it, then why not you? Hidden as they may be, your dragons are there waiting to be discovered, dissolved, and transformed.

When you begin your journey, you will feel the freeing transformation expand within you and it will radiate in a contagious way. This radiance will touch others and you will begin to see miracles happen. As you progress, new understandings will come to you and you will let go of the past. This is exactly the development of your own enlightenment.

> *"One does not become enlightened by imagining figures of light, but by making the darkness conscious."*
>
> ~ Carl Jung

> *"Your task is not to seek for love, but merely to seek and find all the barriers within yourself that you have built against it."*
>
> ~ Rumi

Reprogramming Your Subconscious

When meditating you will arrive at a place in your consciousness where you will come in contact with your own bliss. When you reach this blissful state, you will have no thoughts, no internal chatter, and no agendas – you will just experience your true self in your subconscious realm.

Anytime you *are* thinking, you are operating in the conscious realm. What I am asking you to do is to go to the place where these two meet. From this place, you can do immensely important work.

If you are searching for understanding or want to manifest a certain outcome, form your exploratory question or a specific outcome you wish to manifest and keep it in your conscious mind, but put it to the side momentarily. Using the meditative techniques already mentioned, go to your Spiritual Center. Now ask your question or state your creative intention and just let it be. After a short while, you can repeat this again. You are not looking for answers at this point; you just want to insert your question or intention into your subconscious mind.

By activating your subconscious in this way, you will generate the answers or outcomes shortly. The results will come to you in a variety of ways, either serendipitously when you least expect it, or will be made obvious during further contemplation, or appear symbolically in your dreams.

Once you have determined the correction you want to make,

decide what new self-images you want to implant into your subconscious. Next, create your specific mantra or intention that will override these incorrect images that you want to replace. Then go to your Spiritual Center by meditating and become connected to the deepest part of your own true being.

You might create a mantra to bring about a new opportunity or specific event you want to manifest in the near future. This could be a new job that is more rewarding, finding the perfect mate so you can have the relationship you've always wanted, finding the perfect new home, or whatever you feel will be the next best step for you on your path towards happiness.

By going into your Spiritual Center (your subconscious mind) and then stating your intention (which is retrieved from your conscious mind), you are in the place where your subconscious mind and conscious mind meet and exchange information. You are transitioning into the conscious realm just long enough to retrieve your intention, and then carrying it into your subconscious and putting it out there for the collective unconscious to process, and for your subconscious to assimilate.

The entire energetic universe is a compilation of All that is, and you are now interconnected and communicating with it. You are now cocreating and bringing new things into your life. You are now in the realm of creation and it is you, that is in fact, doing the creating.

In your personal subconscious, this new picture or intention will beneficially override and replace the old, detrimental one. Whatever affirmation you choose, be it to improve something about your internal picture, forgiving others so you can move on and create, or for accepting past events for what they truly were, transitioning it from your conscious mind to your subconscious mind is the most powerful action you can take to manifest a new future. In addition, by communicating it to the Collective Subconscious, you have the power of the universe working for you. When I talked earlier of manifesting things that at one time seemed practically impossible, this is where they come from.

Once you have implanted the new image into your subconscious, see, hear, and feel how your life will be when these benefits are realized. You can do this in a brief and subtle way during your meditation, but stay mostly in your subconscious by not thinking and transition to the conscious realm in only short, brief excursions. Again, thinking activates the conscious mind and meditation activates the subconscious mind. So don't think too much while you are in your meditative state. Enjoy the bliss and insert your intention selectively.

Being in the future you want to create and living it now, even if it's just for a few moments here and there, builds and strengthens the picture you just inserted into your subconscious. You can do this throughout the day whenever an opportunity to do so presents itself. Live your life as though you are well on your way to achieving the future you want to manifest – see it, hear it, feel it, and be it.

You will need to do this practice on several occasions until the transition to the new you has been realized. Deeply rooted concepts will take longer than shorter ones. Things that you have held for years or decades may take months to replace. Longer and more frequent meditations will result in transitions coming sooner, so be patient and experience the transitions as they come.

During each practice, repeat your mantra with sincerity as many times as you feel necessary. Stay in this place of creation and dismiss the old picture just once, then affirm and reaffirm the new creation. Every time you think about the old, you give it power and let its grip on you live to see another day. The correct process is to disavow the old just once, then overwhelmingly empower the new and you do this by recognizing it as the only possible truth – there is no other.

After reciting your mantra appropriately, add this to your affirmation: "I and the Universe are one. I am connected to All, and All is connected to me. Show me the path that I should be on, and I will show you I have the courage to follow it."

You have now made a pact with the Universe. It will give you the direction you should travel, and you have agreed to use your courage to accomplish that which you desire.

By practicing this technique in your quiet times, you will become increasingly proficient at reprogramming your internal picture, forgiving when needed, and accepting past events while stripping them of any power they may have had over you in the past. You will see events manifest that are right on target with the new *you* that you are actively creating.

If you find yourself interacting in your daily activities and an aspect of the old picture comes up, actively replace it immediately with the new version of yourself that you are intent on manifesting. Again, you can say, "No, that used to be me, but that's not me anymore. Now I'm this way." Then only focus on the new image. Refusing to even think about the old image will starve it of any power and will hasten its demise. You can also add: "I have the power to create, and this new me is the only outcome that I will accept."

"Until you make the unconscious, conscious, it will direct your life and you will call it fate."
~ Carl Jung

"Life isn't about finding yourself. Life is about creating yourself."
~ George Bernard Shaw

"We must let go of the life we have planned, so as to accept the one that is waiting for us."
~ Joseph Campbell

Reflecting on this chapter, I invite you to write down any applicable thoughts, take-aways, or lightbulb moments that your inner-self is realizing and trying to communicate to you:

_____

_____

_____

_____

_____

_____

_____

_____

_____

_____

_____

Rules to Love By

The Possibility of Happiness

A relationship is a place you go to give.

You've probably been told that happiness needs to come from the inside. This is definitely true, once you have secured a safe environment. To develop my point, I'd like for you to think of a terrible situation where one person is verbally and physically abused by another. This could be parent to child, child to parent, spouse to spouse, or friend to friend. You can't just tell the abused person that happiness comes from the inside and it's all up to him or her to be happy with their situation— that would be extremely short-sighted.

We all need to be in a safe environment so we can foster the love that we have to share. This is something each person needs to make available and give to another. The perfect environment would be free from judgement and full of acceptance and encouragement. There would be no hierarchy, but a recognition of shared equality. And also an acceptance of not only who the person is, but who they are meant to be.

If a bad situation cannot be made right, then a completely new restart is likely necessary. Once this is achieved, then your inner work will complete your quest for happiness.

> *"To love oneself is the beginning of a lifelong romance."*
> ~ Oscar Wilde

Freedom to Evolve

I am not the same person I was five years ago, and certainly not the same person I was ten years ago. I have actually evolved quite a bit, and so has Beth!

Applying this fact to our future, I have to admit that we will not be the same persons we are today, five years from now, and certainly not ten years from now. I hope not! We would like to think that we will have grown considerably and will be more advanced in our understanding of the world and all of the life that surrounds us! We both expect this to be quite measurable.

I have to think of this not only with Beth and me, but also with my children, my friends, and my coworkers. Remember Heraclitus said, "Change is the only constant in life." Isn't it so true?

Understanding this, I have to give others the freedom to become who they want to become in the future. Everyone's evolution is an expression of their own unique journey and my part is to be an encouraging friend, being helpful whenever I can.

I can be either an enabler for their growth or a hindrance to their freedom. Which do you think is most likely to lead to a happy, long-term, loving relationship that's full of manifesting the life you want to have?

I also have to claim the same right of freedom and self-destiny for myself. No one can ever reach their true potential for happiness if they are expected to live in a cage, with their growth limited by the domination of another. We should all become whatever our true selves wish to become, and no one should live in an environment that is detrimental to their natural growth for any amount of time.

Do we really offer this freedom to others? Do we offer this unconditionally to others? And do you really claim this for yourself?

Often times you will hear someone who has just ended a long-term relationship exclaim: "It feels so good – I can be myself again!" Of course, the problem started whenever that person went off the rails and stopped being their true self, whether by forfeiting their true self or by allowing another's manipulation to slowly immobilize and derail their natural path of development. We should never stop being our true self nor should we allow anyone else to stop being themselves – that's the beginning of the end. We are all meant to evolve along our own path and sharing this journey together with freedom is a mutually beneficial expression of love.

A person who manipulates or overly-controls another person destroys everything in their wake and never creates or achieves happiness. To compensate for the inner-work needed but not done, they watch their world fall into loneliness and isolation. Love and growth have no chance to flourish in such an environment.

We should encourage others close to us to develop the traits and characteristics that they aspire to have, and help them to dissipate any fears that keep them from manifesting into the person they want to become. Encourage others to dream. Then help them to accomplish their dreams.

> *"Love does not consist of gazing at each other, but in looking outward together in the same direction."*
> – Antoine de Saint-Exupery

Relationships

We speak of unconditional Love, and yes, everyone wants it. How would you define unconditional Love? Would you say it is Love without conditions? Aren't respect, honor, and loyalty conditions? What conditions do you mutually agree to and will you always operate from the base of truthfulness?

Conditions can also be inferred and not verbalized. If you want this, you will have to do this as a prerequisite – I expect this from you. If you don't do this for me, then my response will be like this – every time! Is that any way to live?

Do you think you will achieve unconditional love by participating in a constant struggle for domination and successful manipulation of another? Do you think a successful relationship is merely just getting by and dealing with the repeated challenges every time they make themselves known?

What does giving and receiving freedom mean to you? Can you see yourself being capable of it? What insecurities do you think might be driving such behavior? Going inside should reveal what the underlying causes are.

Do you have sufficient confidence in yourself and in your place in the world to allow the universe to flow as it undoubtedly will anyway? If not, you certainly can.

It's been said that religion is the final barrier that keeps you from having a religious experience. What does this mean? A religious experience is between you and the Divine! Anything that gets between these two, such as religion and its dogmas, creates a barrier to having this true experience.

Setting up conditions that keep you from experiencing unconditional love is exactly the same; it stops you from experiencing that which you desire most. Giving someone the freedom to evolve usually magnifies the things that you were most attracted to in the beginning of your relationship.

I am reminded of a beautiful Pygmy story that comes to us from South Africa. It's called The Bird with the Most Beautiful Song in the Forest. In this story, a boy was walking through the forest and heard the most beautiful song he had ever heard, and had a need to follow the sound to discover its origin. He shortly discovered the beautiful song was coming from a particular bird, and he asked this bird to come home with him. When he returned to his house, he asked his father to let the bird join them at their meal. The father was annoyed at having to give food to a mere bird, but did so anyway. After the meal, the bird flew away back to the forest.

The next day the boy heard the same beautiful singing in the forest and again brought the bird home for a meal. The father was even more annoyed but again fed the bird, and the bird then returned to the forest.

On the third day, the boy heard the same beautiful singing and again brought the beautiful songbird home for a meal, but this time the father decided enough was enough. Their food was too precious to share with just a bird, so he sent the boy off on an errand.

When the boy had left on his errand, the father took the bird into the forest and killed the bird, and with the bird the song died as well, and with the song the man died. The bird was gone forever, and with the bird, the most beautiful song in the forest was gone forever, and with the song, the man was gone forever.

By limiting anyone from growth, you kill the song. If you kill the song, how can you expect anything of value to be created? It was most likely the song that first attracted you in the beginning.

Love is about expansion and participation in something that is bigger than ourselves. Letting go is about trusting, and not only trusting in yourself or in your partner, but in trusting in life itself; it's how the universe works. This is the only way the song can flourish and be continually appreciated.

How would you define your relationships? What are your core values when it comes to relating to others? Have you taken the time to decide what guideposts you will use for your navigation? If you were to choose just three words to describe your moral compass, and this moral compass is what you will use to guide you in all areas of your life, what would those three words be?

These are personal answers and will differ for almost everyone. When I did this, I came up with Love, Kindness, and Freedom. These represent the three most important areas that will give me a meaningful experience of life. You may find other words that will better describe what is most important to you and your partner. It's up to you to decide what you truly want to keep as your moral compass.

Everyone wants and needs Love in their life to make living worthwhile. Kindness was also fairly easy. Who wants to live in an environment that doesn't equally share kindness? If you're with the right person, I even think kindness breeds happiness. For the third word to describe how I wanted our relationship to be, I had many thoughts; adventure, as we both like to travel, see new places and do new things; fun, as that is really a necessary part of enjoying life and makes everything pleasurable; serving others, as this speaks strongly to our altruistic side; and security, both emotional and financial, as emotional security gives you the "knowing" and financial security delivers you from the worry and "unknowing" that can really take its toll on any relationship.

The word Freedom encompassed more of the facets that I considered most important in how I want to have my relationship with Beth, and also be treated myself. For me, Freedom includes adventure, so we are free to travel and do what we want when we want. Freedom is also somewhat synonymous with fun and pleasure. It has always been really important to me that each of us are free to not only be who we are now, but that we both have the freedom to become whoever we might choose to become as we both continually evolve. To me, Freedom also includes a solid base where altruism and security can exist, grow, and thrive.

I encourage you, whether by yourself or with a partner, to come up with the three words that will best describe the moral compass that will keep you on track and act as your North Star. Share them with each other and explain why they are important to you. Commit these to memory and use them to guide you through your evolutionary processes.

> *"Every heart sings a song incomplete, until another heart whispers back. Those who wish to sing always find a song. At the touch of a lover, everyone becomes a poet."*
>
> ~ Plato

Honest Emotional Ownership and Releasing the Ego

Equally value and respect each other's emotional ownership.

Beth and I have agreed that if we have a decision to make and we have opposing thoughts as far as the course of action we should take, we will ask each other how important this is on a scale from one to ten. If it is an eight on her scale and a five on mine, then the decision will be the way Beth wants it to be because it is more important to her than it is to me.

If the need for another decision arises and again we have different thoughts as to the directions we should take, if it's a seven on my scale and a five on hers, then we go with the outcome I would prefer to see, because it is more important to me.

This allows us both to see our most desired outcomes manifest, and to know that we are choosing our path equally and together. It is also very rewarding to let your partner know that you care about them so much that small petty things have no power whatsoever when compared to the love and admiration you have for each other.

This makes it really easy to get along. All you have to do is give up the ego's tendency to want to always win and have it your way. In the end, you have the most beautiful love you could ever imagine, and all of the other small things fade into the past without even leaving a trace. I can't even remember the things I yielded to Beth one year ago, I only know that we both really enjoy being with each other.

What does it matter if we go to this restaurant or that one tonight, or go hiking on this trail or another one? In the big picture, most things we hang on to are really trivial. Our egos hang on to the weirdest things, and can destroy that which we are seeking the most.

Love, being easy, and having mutual respect and admiration for each other is what will deliver the most beautiful relationship you can imagine. Domination and control will stifle and smother life's energy, whereas freedom, honesty, and respect will expand life's energy.

Our decision making process is extremely valuable in our

relationship because it not only builds trust, but exercises openness, honesty, and respect on a regular basis. This promotes mutual growth and admiration.

Beth and I agree on most things, so it's not like we pull out this tool multiple times per day. When we do have opposing views, both of us know how important the choice is to each other. Discussing the options honestly and communicating in a heartfelt way brings us closer on many levels.

With relationships, you can go far deeper with another person by fostering a willingness to understand rather than acting out your life in a defensive drama, which only leaves the other person distanced and disoriented. All relationships are here to teach us something, and often the lesson is an internal one.

When I was teaching my ten-year old son how to drive my truck around the back part of our twenty-acre ranch, there was one day when he wanted to go do some chores (that he just happened to need the truck for – go figure!) When he was backing up he accidentally backed into the house and put a dent in the aluminum siding that was really noticeable. He thought he was done for; he really thought the worst.

I did my best to keep from smiling, so as not to be too dismissive on the importance of the mistake, and asked him "What are you doing?" He did his best to explain that he was looking elsewhere to the place he wanted to go and didn't look behind him while the vehicle was still backing up. I told him how important it is to be more careful and to always look before and while your vehicle is moving. He assured me of how bad he felt and that he would always know what was around him anytime he was ever in a moving vehicle, and that was the end of it. He told me later in his adulthood that he didn't think he was going to live to see another day. Instead, he saw compassion, understanding, acceptance, and love.

About five years later, we moved off the property, and three years after that a renter accidentally burnt the house to the ground (with the dented siding still in-place). Luckily, no one was hurt in the accidental fire. By the way, the truck eventually ended up in the scrap yard. Lesson is: Don't sweat the small stuff because in the end, stuff doesn't really matter, only Love does.

> *"Love does not claim possession, but gives freedom."*
> ~ Rabindranath Tagore

> *"Now love ought to be for the advantage of both parties, and for the injury of neither."*
> ~ Phaedrus…in dialog with Plato

> *"The love that I cannot command is not mine; let me not disturb myself about it, nor attempt to filch it from its rightful owner. A heart that I supposed mine has drifted and gone. Shall I go in pursuit? Shall I forcibly capture the truant and transfix it with the barb of my selfish affection, and pin it to the wall of my character? Rather let me leave my doors and windows open, intent only on living so nobly that the best cannot fail to be drawn to me by an irresistible attraction."*
> ~ Victoria C. Woodhall November 20, 1871

Forgiveness and Empowered Acceptance

Unless we release all of our emotional ties that bind us negatively to the past and hold us back, we will not be free to create the connected and loving self we should be pursuing.

Forgiveness is the key to freedom from our past. It is also necessary to manifest the person we want to become. This is not to say we should forget the past or to pretend it didn't happen, but rather to acknowledge that everything in space and time has its reason for being here – to teach us something. We are all a part of the evolution of humankind, and we all partake in this process on a daily basis.

What is it that we can learn from our past experiences?

Difficulties often come to offer us the chance to learn something we need, so we can progress further in our personal evolution. If we have encountered sorrow, pain, or abuse, we can be in a better position to know joy when it comes and show more compassion to others in need.

If you let the sorrow from the past continually have its hooks in you, it's like being in a boat that is securely tied to the dock. You may wish to set sail and have a joyous and adventurous life, but you just can't seem to get started; every time you look around you still haven't gone anywhere. Let the lessons of the past empower you to move forward with a stronger resolve to create your future self.

We create our thoughts and out of our thoughts come our actions, and our actions influence the entire direction of our lives. Whenever thoughts are stuck in the past, we generate actions based on the past and secretly live in the past over and over again. Therefore, our thoughts are at the root of everything we manifest. Creation happens in the present, in the now, with an eye to the future. Decide what you want in your life, disempower any past trauma, and begin creating the future you envision – today.

The Invitation

It doesn't interest me what you do for a living.
I want to know what you ache for and if you dare to
dream of meeting your heart's longing.

It doesn't interest me how old you are.
I want to know if you will risk looking like a fool for
love, for your dream, for the adventure of being alive.

It doesn't interest me what planets are squaring
your moon.

I want to know if you have touched the center of your own sorrow, if you have been opened by life's betrayals or have become shriveled and closed from fear of further pain.

I want to know if you can sit with pain, mine or your own, without moving to hide it or fade it or fix it.

I want to know if you can be with joy, mine or your own, if you can dance with wildness and let the ecstasy fill you to the tips of your fingers and toes without cautioning us to be careful, to be realistic, to remember the limitations of being human.

It doesn't interest me if the story you are telling me is true. I want to know if you can disappoint another to be true to yourself; if you can bear the accusation of betrayal and not betray your own soul; if you can be faithless and therefore trustworthy.

I want to know if you can see Beauty even when it is not pretty, every day, and if you can source your own life from its presence.

I want to know if you can live with failure, yours and mine, and still stand at the edge of the lake and shout to the silver of the full moon, "Yes!"

It doesn't interest me to know where you live or how much money you have. I want to know if you can get up, after the night of grief and despair, weary and bruised to the bone and do what needs to be done to feed the children.

Dennis A. Belanger

It doesn't interest me who you know or how you came to be here. I want to know if you will stand in the center of the fire with me and not shrink back.

It doesn't interest me where or what or with whom you have studied. I want to know what sustains you, from the inside, when all else falls away.

I want to know if you can be alone with yourself and if you truly like the company you keep in the empty moments.[1]

> ~ Oriah Mountain Dreamer

---

[1] By Oriah "Mountain Dreamer" House from her book, THE INVITATION© 1999. Published by HarperONE, San Francisco. All rights reserved. Presented with permission of the author. www.oriah.org

Reflecting on this chapter, I invite you to write down any applicable thoughts, take-aways, or lightbulb moments that your inner-self is realizing and trying to communicate to you:

_____

_____

_____

_____

_____

_____

_____

_____

_____

_____

_____

_____

All the Best is Waiting for You

Plan Your Work, Work Your Plan

If you haven't already, you should write down the things you want to manifest in your life. This will be your roadmap to the future.

Generally, a five-year forecast will give you plenty to work towards and focus on, but in some cases, you may have a much larger goal that extends out to ten years or more. You can change or update your list as you start manifesting things and see the new possibilities as they make themselves known.

The following exercise of creating a five-year plan will help determine what is really important to you, or both of you, if you are doing this with your partner.

First, get one or two full-size notepads and pens that are comfortable to write with. You will be listing everything that you want to manifest in your life and allocating a time for each goal to be realized.

The guidelines to this exercise are that there are no wrong entries, and nothing is too big or too small. You don't have to know how you will accomplish anything at this point, just write as quickly as you can in a free-flow manner, listing all the things that you would like to manifest in your life.

What matters most is that you list the things you really want to manifest for your own personal reasons, and not because you think it might be cool to own a beach-house on Maui...you must really want one in order for it to be a valid entry on your list.

If you knew a magic Genie was going to pop out of a bottle and grant everything you have on your list – what would *that* list look like? The crucial idea here is not to be limited by any hidden inhibitions or self-doubts. Everything exists as a possibility for you to have and achieve, so reach deep and let it all out! This is your first step in manifesting what you truly desire.

When creating your list of the things you want to manifest, list different categories as headers before you start. You may have full pages or half pages with headings on the top such as:

- **Personal Goals** – What type of fitness, health, emotional healing, etc., do you want to learn, improve on, or achieve? Do you want to learn Tai Chi or yoga, write a book, take art classes, or start a hobby or craft? Would you like to travel to the places you have always dreamed of going to?
- **Educational Goals** – What do you need to learn to be the person you want to become? What intellectual endeavors interest you? Are you interested in learning a foreign language, finance and accounting, or mastering investing principals?
- **Financial Goals** – How much monthly or annual income do you want – how much exactly? What investment types and how much value do you want in your future real estate and stock portfolios? What job or industry do you want to work in? Do you want to send your kids to college and not worry about the cost? What do you want your net worth to be and at what age do you want to reach financial independence?
- **Spiritual Goals** – What level of spirituality do you want to develop – how and what type? Would you like to teach others? What do you want to practice and experience on a regular basis?

- **Material Goals** – Would you like to build or buy your dream home, own a vacation home, have a sports car or a boat? Yes, these are all ok!
- **Relationship Goals** – Do you want to find the perfect relationship, free yourself from an unwanted relationship, or repair a damaged relationship? What would your perfect relationship look like? What could you learn or how could you change in order to become a better partner?
- **Giving Back** – How will you help others, both now and in the future, who may be struggling in life and who may be able to learn or benefit from your developed wisdom? What will you do to return a portion of what you have received, or will receive, back to those who could benefit from your assistance? What will you do to leave your mark on the world and make the world a better place?
- **Additional Goals** – Are there any other categories that may be of interest to you?

Next, is to move quickly once you start listing your items – don't get caught up in the details, you already know the details so just write in your own version of short-hand. You'll be able to add the details once you've finished the exercise. It's important to continue the uninterrupted free flow of ideas as they are being recorded onto your notepad. So don't over-think or over-analyze, just free-flow everything you would like to manifest in your life.

If you are doing this exercise with a partner, it is best if you do this individually and compare notes after you have completed your individualized lists. You can combine your two lists easily and come up with a joint "Master Plan" if you choose.

Once you have completed your list, write a number next to each item that represents when you will accomplish this task – one year, two years, three years, etc. You may have some larger tasks that will take longer to manifest, say ten years, in which case you will write the number ten next to these items if applicable.

Next, reorganize your list by combining all categories together and by grouping all of the one-year goals together, two-year goals together, etc., (and incorporate both lists together if you are doing it with a partner and making a team plan). You may recognize some in-between steps that are needed to transition, such as if you are going to sell your house in one state and build a new house in another state, where will you be staying when you sell your current house and before you build the new house? Fill in any gaps.

Once you have categorized all of your goals into their yearly designations according to when you will be accomplishing them, sort each group in order of importance, listing your most important goal first. Then list your top-five most important one-year goals in the space provided in the appendix section in the back of this book. Do the same for your second-year goals, third-year, etc.

You now have your five 'most important' goals identified and listed for each of the next five years. This is a complete roadmap to get you to the lifestyle you want to live. This is your own personal contract with yourself. Share it with others if you wish, or keep it for your own viewing. Do look at it often and plan your efforts for accomplishments on a daily and weekly basis.

Knowing what you want is crucial to manifesting what you want. Five goals for each year will be sufficient as long as they are large, important to you, and obtainable if you put forth the needed effort.

On your larger goals, break them down into the smaller accomplishments needed to achieve the final goal. If you want to be at this place in five years, where will you need to be in four years? How about in three years, or two years? You should pace yourself into success, and not leave it all to be done in the final year.

Reading your list of intentions and expectations repeatedly over time is really powerful in and of itself. By doing this you are embedding it into your Personal Subconscious, and this of course, is connected to the Collective Subconscious. Every time you read your list, you are making incremental progress by programming your unconscious, which is where manifesting culminates.

Sometimes the requested outcome you cast from your intentions will come to you in a different way and won't be seen until a short time later.

A personal example I can offer is when Beth and I decided to purchase land in Washington State. Our plan was to build our perfect dream home and retire there four years later. After projecting our intentions with the utmost clarity and countless times, we researched and found many promising properties.

After three trips to Washington to view the selected properties and meeting with our local Realtor, nothing was even close to what we had envisioned. If the land was beautiful, the road noise from the interstate eliminated any chance of tranquility. In many cases, the pictures weren't accurate and we got to the listed property only to be completely disappointed. "What's up with this manifesting stuff? Why isn't it working?"

Beth and I returned home and after three scouting trips, each trip being seven to ten days, we were left wondering if our little piece of paradise would ever be found. One month later we found a really nice investment property close to home in Colorado, and then another property that was unbelievably excellent (And I do mean unbelievably!!!) and we purchased both of them – four months apart from each other – and now we are in a much better position and can even "up" the price that we originally had as our budget for the new property. You see, the universe can understand the outcome you want to achieve even though your initial plan to get there may be underdeveloped and flawed. You will still manifest your desired outcome and the wisdom of the process will be revealed to you along the way.

It may take a little more time but we are not in a hurry. We also now understand with more clarity what we want and are in a much better position to manifest it when the time is right, rather than jumping too soon with our enthusiasm blazing. So, go figure.

The universe has a way of working things out for the best if our hearts are in the right place and our intentions are strong, clear, and communicated well.

When our intentions are manifested in a different way that is actually better, it's just the universe knowing what we really want, even if we don't see what's best at the time we're asking. You will know this for yourself if you practice the techniques I've mentioned and you take this journey.

If you question how good you could possibly have it (caused by incorrect societal programming or autonomic conditioning) just think about those who rose from poverty and tough times and excelled to greatness. Many of them started with nothing but determination and a will to succeed in their endeavors, and many of them have even changed the world.

Once you have your plan, look at every action you take, because every action will be taking you either closer or further away from achieving your goals…expediting them or delaying them. This is an excellent way to decide what actions you will take for any given situation.

What will you need to know to accomplish each goal you have listed? What other things will you need to know to accomplished your larger goals? Do you already have these skill sets developed or are there a couple of gaps you need to fill in? Start working on the development of your future self now – it's all part of the process of getting there.

By studying the things you need to learn you are setting yourself up to succeed. By focusing on your goals, learning what you need to know, and by projecting your envisioned intentions to the universe… how could you not succeed? You can manifest anything you wish – it's all up to you!

How do you spend your time? If you want to achieve something, and you find you have an extra thirty minutes, should you watch TV or read something in your field of interest? You will see that it is your determination and communicated intentions that combine to create a force that is practically unstoppable.

Time is the only thing that is truly limited. Money can come and go, love and relationships can come and go, even health and illness can come and go, but once time goes, there is no getting it back. So spend your time wisely and be in control of your own destiny. You are the only one that will manifest the life you want to have.

Offer kindness and respect every time you speak. Be the person you want to become. There is no need to wait for the future to get here. Your future is always starting right now and will quickly turn into your past. So now is the time to act. Start living your future, as well as being your future – now!

> *"I learned this, at least, from my experiment: that if one advances confidently in the direction of his dreams, and endeavors to live the live he has imagined, he will meet with a success unexpected in the common hours.*
>
> *He will put some things behind, will pass an invisible boundary; new, universal, more liberal laws will begin to establish themselves around and within him; or the old laws will be expanded, and interpreted in his favor in a more liberal sense, and he will live with the license of a higher order of beings.*
>
> *In proportion as he simplifies his life, the laws of the universe will seem less complex, and solitude will not be solitude, nor poverty poverty, nor weakness weakness. If you have built castles in the air, your work need not be lost; that is where they should be. Now put the foundations under them."*
>
> – Henry David Thoreau – Walden (1854)

> *"Ultimately, that is the definition of bravery: Not being afraid of yourself."*
>
> ~ Chogram Trungpa

> *"What lies behind you and what lies in front of you, pales in comparison to what lies inside of you."*
>
> ~ Ralph Waldo Emerson

Self-Learning and Achievement

In Buddhism, a Bodhisattva is a person whose highly developed spirituality illuminates others. You can, in your own way, be a Bodhisattva, and have a highly positive impact on all those around you.

What lessons and what learning have already come to you? What future lessons will the universe bring into your pathway? Whether they seem to be good or bad events, it is always learning that awaits. If you catch yourself rehashing events from the past that you have no ability to change or learn from, stop wasting your mental energy and start thinking about how you will design your future. Past unproductive patterns will get you nowhere; the current and future patterns you create can change your life.

Dream big, you have nothing stopping you other than yourself. Plan what you want by writing your action plan. Then take the necessary action and bring your dreams into reality. Learn to meditate, experience your Spiritual Center, connect with the All in the Universe that is within you, release your empowered intentions from that place, and manifest the life you want to have and share.

> *"There are only two ways to live your life. One is as though nothing is a miracle. The other is as though everything is a miracle."*
>
> ~ Albert Einstein

"It is not the critic who counts; not the man who points out how the strong man stumbles, or where the doer of deeds could have done them better. The credit belongs to the man who is actually in the arena, whose face is marred by dust and sweat and blood; who strives valiantly; who errs, who comes short again and again, because there is no effort without error and shortcoming; but who does actually strive to do the deeds; who knows great enthusiasms, the great devotions; who spends himself in a worthy cause; who at the best knows in the end the triumph of high achievement, and who at the worst, if he fails, at least fails while daring greatly, so that his place shall never be with those cold and timid souls who neither know victory nor defeat."

~ Theodore Roosevelt

Manifesting Financial Independence

We all have different ideas about money and wealth. Some think it's unattainable, some think that it's evil, and others realize it gives you both options and freedom to do what you want as well as giving you freedom from worry. It can also allow you to be monetarily charitable and help others.

If you live in a capitalistic society, there are certain rules of the game that have been set up to play by, and whether you think them fair or unfair does not negate their existence – they do exist and will likely continue to exist regardless of your views or opinions about them.

I look at money as a multiplier of who you are as an individual. If Mother Theresa had received a few extra million dollars in her lifetime the world would probably still be reaping the benefits, however, a few extra million in the hands of an evil person or a drug addict would likely lead to a disastrous outcome. What good would you do for the world if you were in a position of financial independence? It is who you are as a person that gets amplified when you become financially independent.

If you want to make the world a better place, or for now, just make your own world a better place, having many options versus limited options will definitely be helpful. Yes, Mother Theresa accomplished great things for humanity without becoming wealthy, but she gathered wealth and redirected it so it could be put to better use, and expressed her Godlike devotion for the entire world to see.

Although this book is not a book about investments or building wealth, nor is it a book about what will make you happy – as that is for you to figure out by going "inside" and finding your true self – it is a book on manifesting what you want in your life. This leads me to suspect that financial independence may have crossed your mind at some time, so I'd like to share how I achieved this and let you know that anyone, anywhere, can do the same.

I've talked with others in the past about this topic of financial independence and I most often hear "I'd like to do that someday, but I can't right now." Therefore, they never take a first step of any kind and even years later are still continuing to struggle.

Lao Tzu wrote in the *Tao Te Ching*: "A journey of a thousand miles begins with a single step." So what's your reason for never starting?

If you have this mentality and are waiting for the right time to come, it most likely will never come. The right time is when you agree to take your first step, then tell yourself you will keep going and not stop until you are comfortably where you want to be.

A good first step may be analyzing where you are right now, making an action plan, and learning the things in the areas where your knowledge may be lacking. What will you need on your journey to financial independence that you don't have now? You can always take this first step of organizing, learning, and planning "*today*" with very few exceptions.

You've heard the saying that "Knowledge is Power"; well, knowledge without action is pretty useless. It's the action that materializes the Power. What if Edison or Tesla never organized their workshops, but rather only daydreamed as they looked out their windows? What if Pablo Picasso never picked up a paintbrush but rather only thought about what he could do with one? There would be no creation of power and the world would likely be a very different place.

If you want to find a better job, sitting under a tree and wishing for it might be a good first step, but the universe will want to see action – like brushing up your resume and searching the online job boards – before it grants you your wish.

Manifesting, which is what this book is all about, needs action to be taken, both spiritually and physically, in order to bring about the change you want to have and experience. Keep Lao Tzu's wisdom close to you and take the action you need to take. It's the only way to move forward.

If you continue to learn and improve, and project your intentions from your Spiritual Center, you will achieve your goals with stunning regularity. Your manifesting will bring you achievements that you never previously thought possible, and this will lead to even more and greater accomplishments.

Much of what we dream of having is, in fact, possible. We may not currently have the needed information to take things to the next level, but it is always available. So take action; it's the one option you have under your control and is the most important first step to manifesting the life you want.

There are only two ways of building wealth: labor and capital.

Labor is earning money in exchange for physical work (I will dig a trench for you and you will pay me $50). Capital is earning money in exchange for the use of investment funds (I will loan you $100 and you will pay me back $120 within a specific amount of time). You can work for money, which is limited by your physical condition and time (age), or you can have your money work to bring you more money, which is not limited by your physical condition nor by time.

Earning wealth by labor is limited by the amount of labor

you can produce. Earning wealth by capital is limited only to how much capital you have to invest. By learning to invest properly, your amount of capital will continue to increase with time and easily outpace any wealth gained from your labor.

We all can do one or the other, or preferably both. Relying on labor will diminish your capacity to earn income as the years go by. Relying on capital to build wealth will increase handsomely over time, providing you know the rules of the game.

You probably know that the historical statistics for creating a successful business are not good. Ninety percent of all new businesses fail in the first five years, and of those remaining after the first five years, ninety percent of those fail in the following five years. So, you have a 1% chance of being successful and a 99% chance of losing all of your investment capital.

Investing in stocks can be lucrative over time and there are many good books to read on this subject. I would recommend "The Intelligent Investor" by Benjamin Graham, first published in 1949. Warren Buffet first read this book when he was 20 years old and still calls it "By far the best book on investing ever written."

You can watch YouTube videos of interviews with Warren Buffet plus a host of other videos that will facilitate your learning. Definitely educate yourself and play with 'pretend money' before you play with real cash.

With stock investing, I always think of the quote from the great hockey player Wayne Gretzky. When asked why he was such a great hockey player, he replied: "I skate to where the puck is going to be." So with stocks, I ask myself what companies and what industries will experience huge growth over the next five years? This had led me to green energy (solar, electric vehicles, the battery companies that will supply electric vehicles, 5G Networks, etc.) and tech stocks. At the beginning of our industrial age, manufacturing companies such as General Electric and General Motors grew to become behemoth organizations. Now in the age of tech, companies like Apple, Google, Microsoft, and Amazon dwarf them. Which companies will be in the next circle of superstars? Will they be from the Green Energy Sector and Autonomous Driving Vehicles? What about the next round of support companies that will supply the electronics, 3-D manufacturing, or Solid State Battery Technology (SSBT) needed by the next generation of global companies? I am completely satisfied with my realized growth in these areas.

On the other hand, more millionaires have been made with real estate investing than in any other industry. It is fairly easy to do if you are willing to learn what you need to know and are willing to take your first step.

Just imagine if you bought a few properties ten years ago, how much would they be worth today compared to what you would have bought them for? If you wait another ten years, what would you expect the selling price to be? That financial gain can either be yours or belong to some other investor. In this example, we are only talking about appreciation, which is only one way you can gain wealth from real estate.

If you were to tell me that you can't afford to invest or to buy your first house that you really would like to have, I would tell you to figure out what you need to do so that you can start investing, say, one year from now. However, you really need to take action to do what needs to be done and not just let the upcoming year come and go without addressing your investment shortcomings.

If you say you can't accomplish this, let me ask you a question: If there was an economic downturn of some sort, and you found yourself making $5,000 less per year compared to your usual income, would you be able to find a way to make it work? You would likely reply: "Well, yes, I'd figure out a way to make it work because I would have to."

So just make believe that is happening now and you will save $5,000 per year. And if you do, how much will you have in 3 years? $15,000? No! You should have $19,965 if you have invested and let your money make you more money (at a 10% return each year). That's enough for a down payment to purchase a $390,000 house to use as your personal residence! Now you are on your way!

If you're thinking that making that kind of mortgage payment might be difficult, rent out an extra room or two and now because of your housemates, you are in the rental business. You can use this rental income to pay for most of, or all of, your mortgage.

In most regions, your house should go up in value by an average 5% per year, or $19,500 per year (See Appreciation Rates table covering 2009 through 2019 – 60.8% over ten years, or an average of 6.08% each year for all homes sold in the U.S.)

If you connect with a Realtor® they can set you up with a property search by a company like CoreLogic® that will tell you the previous selling prices and you can calculate the previous appreciation rates for the properties in your area that you are considering. You can then estimate if you think your area is growing or stagnating and decide if you think the past appreciation rate will slow down, stay the same, or increase. Either way, I've found a 5% appreciation rate is a good long-term rate to use for consideration and calculation.

On a $390,000 purchase, that appreciation amounts to almost $20,000 in wealth building each year that you didn't have before. Remember, your down payment was only $19,965, so you got all of your wealth back in one year and now you have an extra $20,000 accumulating per year (which will increase by the effects of compounding each year) for the rest of your life!

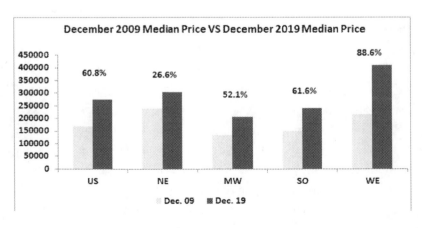

Once you get your first house, after two or three years you should be able to purchase another home and use your first as a rental. Now you have two homes, one paying for itself and giving you a healthy profit, and your newest home that you live in. With 5% appreciation on both properties your wealth accumulation from appreciation should be somewhere around $35,000.00 per year. Think about how much you will earn if you continue to build your investment portfolio to include five properties. The value of your assets should grow easily by $87,500 per year from appreciation, not to mention your positive cash flow, which should be at least $10,000 per year per unit, or an additional $50,000 for all five units just from the cash flow. That's $137,500 per year in wealth building without considering how fast your tenants are paying off your mortgages at no cost to you (mortgage buy down). You can see where this will take you in ten years, can't you? Yes, to financial independence!

If it takes you ten years to get to this point – so what! You will have created a real estate portfolio that will give you plenty of options as well as a really secure retirement. So do what you need to do to learn how to invest successfully in real estate. Remember, without action you are likely to never advance your position or gain financial independence.

Let's look a little closer at the three ways investment real estate increases your wealth. We mentioned the first already, and that's appreciation. Over the long run, most appreciation rates have averaged 5% per year. In hot markets where prices are rising fast, your properties can increase in value by up to 9 or 10% (I've experienced this myself). A $400,000 home should sell for at least $510,000 five years later and more than $651,557 in ten years.

Where this really comes into play is if you have several properties. Let's say over the course of ten years you have acquired five rental properties, and each property is worth $400,000. That's $2 million worth of real estate and someone else is paying off the mortgages for you plus you get to keep the excess income as cash flow. Let's say your properties collectively appreciate at 5% per year. That's $100,000 each year for you – and this is just from appreciation. Where will you be in another ten years? Probably on a beach or at a mountain resort!

The second way real estate investing will make you financially independent is with its positive cash flow. This is the excess of gross rental income less your other expenses like mortgages, taxes, insurance, and any other utilities, repairs, or maintenance costs you may choose to pay. This should amount to a minimum of $10,000 per rental per year for smaller investments. So if you work your portfolio up to five properties you should have anywhere from $50,000 to $85,000, depending on the size of your properties, as additional income.

The third way you build wealth with real estate is by the Mortgage-Buy-Down. On rental properties, the gross rent you collect will be more than enough to pay your property mortgage, taxes, and insurance, (plus extra for you – positive cash flow). Every month the balance of your mortgage debt is reduced by the amount of principal payments made on your loan to the bank by your tenants. This increases your equity (and wealth) with every payment made, and the longer you have a loan, more of the payment is dedicated to principal and less to the monthly interest you pay – it's like a sliding scale that favors the bank in the beginning and increasingly favors you as time goes on. This means the longer you own a property the faster the mortgage is paid off – just don't refinance or you go back to square-one. (Have you ever wondered why banks are so happy to refinance your loan?)

You can go online and print an amortization schedule for free with your numbers in it, and this will show you over time how fast this adds up. Eventually your tenants will pay off the entire loan and all of the rental income (less taxes and insurance) will be all yours! How's that for a retirement plan?

Here is how I calculate a real estate deal to see if it's worth pursuing. If you take the sale price of a property, then subtract the down payment, currently 5% if you are going to live in the property you're looking at purchasing, 20% if it is a non-owner occupied single family residential property, or 25% if it is a multi-family rental property that you will not be living in. This will give you the loan amount needed to finalize the purchase.

Your mortgage payment can be easily calculated by searching Google for a mortgage calculator and putting in the loan amount, the current interest rate that banks are quoting you, and your credit score. This will tell you what your principal and interest payment will be.

Add the taxes and insurance, and any other expenses, all of which is disclosed on the real estate listing, to your principle and interest payment. Now you know your monthly costs to operate and the total costs to purchase (not counting the bank fees and prepaid expenses to close the loan, which you can get from any banker).

The current rental information for the property will be stated on the listing, and you can compare this income to the monthly expenses you just calculated and you will know what your approximate monthly cash flow is likely to be. Sometimes the existing rents are lower than they should be, so there may be opportunity to increase them over time to the market rate. Craigslist® will tell you what the current rents are for comparable properties.

If you calculate your annual income from cash flow (monthly cash flow already calculated x 12) then add in your gain from appreciation (generally 5% of the overall property value), plus the amount of mortgage buy down from the amortization table, you end up with what I call Total Wealth Accumulation. This is how much you will grow your wealth in one year.

I've included a worksheet for these calculations in the appendix that will show the flow of information in an easy-to-understand format.

One aspect of purchasing real estate that is often overlooked is buying down the interest rate. This can be to your advantage if you plan to keep your properties for five years or more, and there is no sense of leaving money on the table – especially when it's your money!

Your banker will tell you the actual cost of buying down the interest rate. This calculation is how to look at it, although the numbers I'm using are dependent on the loan amount, the current interest rates, and your local bank fees, so input the current data for your area.

Let's say you want to buy down the interest rate from 4.5% to 3.75%, a savings of ¾ of a point over the entire life of the loan. The current cost for this at my local bank is $7,400, but it will lower the monthly mortgage payment by $152 per month because of the lower interest rate. By dividing the $7,400 total cost to do this by my monthly savings of $152, you can see that you will recover your buy-down cost of $7,400 in 48.7 months ($7400/$152 per month = 48.68 months) or just over four years. That means you get your $7,400 back in approximately four years and then save (earn) an extra $152 per month, each month, for however long you have this mortgage. That's $1,824 per year or $18,240 for every ten years, and this is going right into your pocket.

If you have any questions about qualifying for a mortgage or on any applicable first-time-buyer programs that makes owning real estate easier, you can talk with a banker, and they will let you know where you need to be in order to buy your first home or investment property. Do shop the banks and credit unions – some have much better loan packages!

I have a friend who decided to take this advice, talked with a banker, and made a game plan to get his financial house in order. One year later, he bought his first house and he is now proudly enjoying owning his first home. He has in his 5-year plan a goal to purchase his second property in two years. You can do this too!

There are a few other things to know in order to become proficient at investing and markets will definitely vary throughout different parts of the country. And there will be times when it's better to buy and other times when it will be better to wait until better buys are available.

Studying markets and the profits you can make is the best way to become proficient, and anybody can do this at any time by just running the numbers and seeing what current conditions offer. You can read real estate investment books or watch YouTube videos. All the information you need is readily available.

College rentals, Airbnb's, single family homes, multi-family apartments, small office buildings, or storage buildings, are just some of the areas you can specialize in and there are plenty of good books available to learn what you need to know for each of these categories. This may seem far-fetched but it is not – many have done it, even starting out from humble beginnings just like I did. This may not seem to be spiritual, but it is!

The Universe makes it available to you as one of the choices you have and if you are thinking that Abundance *should be* a part of your life then take the necessary steps and make it happen – it is just one of the things you are free to manifest if you so choose.

If you think that you don't deserve Abundance I would suggest you look inside, find your Center, sort through your Dragons as discussed earlier, and create the Life that is waiting for you. Once you start on the journey of improving, the sky's the limit. This is exactly what I did and now I am available to help others.

Ask yourself: "If I want my life to be full of abundance and good options, then what will I need to know that I don't know now?" Then begin learning what you need to know to overcome any educational shortcomings you discover. Nobody knows everything, so it's not even a humbling experience, it's more of an honest experience.

Take action by developing your ability to meditate and connecting to the greater consciousness, and learn the things that you need to know to become successful.

I did this first by using the library and then buying books on my Kindle. Like everything, once you start going down a particular road you will meet like-minded people who seem to just show up. Like attracts like! One thing leads to another and soon you will look around and realize you've made the life you previously only dreamt about. It is available to everyone, so long as you take action and do the work that is required.

Whether it is financial abundance or an abundance of any kind, you have the power to achieve it. Finding your Spiritual Center and being connected to the All is extremely important. Casting out your intentions from your Spiritual Center and asking for guidance will connect you with all the power needed and you will be amazed at what you can accomplish. You decide when to take action and start manifesting – the beginning point is all up to you! It's the conscious mind working with the subconscious mind that develops the plan, and it's the unconscious mind working with the conscious mind that delivers it.

> *"One cannot step into the same river twice.*
> *In the flow of time, an opportunity lost, is lost forever."*
> ~ Heraclitus

Changing Your Game

If you want to change your game – then change your game! Who's in control here anyway? If you aren't in control now, at least like you want to be, then this is the perfect time to take control, and I mean right now!

The 5-year goal plan you just made, lists all of your major goals that will guide you to the major breakthroughs you will manifest. Now it's time to create a second list of smaller things that will get you moving on that path *right now*, so you can see yourself making progress towards the new life you have outlined. Doing so will allow you to build on the smaller successes immediately and will strengthen your sense of progress.

What smaller steps can you do right now that will get you to accomplish your major goals faster? If you had improved health and fitness on your major list, you may want to include stretching, floor exercises, walking, hiking, biking, practicing Tai Chi, or doing yoga for 20 minutes each day. These are all things you can start today! You don't need to wait!

In addition, you could change your diet by giving up what you know isn't good for your physical health and substitute it for something you know will be a much healthier choice. You can do things like this right now – today – and continue it on a regular basis. This will give you the start that you need to be on your path to a better life!

There is no good reason not to, so why not start improving your life right now. If you have educational goals, research what will be the first book you will read to start you on this journey and download it, see if your local library has it (also videos and audiobooks), or go out and buy it today.

This will empower you because you are not only seeing the change, not only participating in the change, but learning that it is you, yourself, that is actively creating and manifesting the change. This is exactly how countless others have accomplished their dreams. So experience the change you want now; it is easily in your power to do so.

When I decided to start eating healthier, I immediately went to the cupboard, pantry, and fridge, and threw out all the foods I knew I no longer wanted to eat. That day I went to the bookstore and looked through all of the health-food cookbooks they had, and bought the two books that appealed to me the most. Then I sat in the car and made a shopping list to cover the first recipes I would make over the next few days. The rest is history! I immediately went vegan and have never looked back. I love the health benefits, the learning, and all of the fun that goes with it. The food that I cook or prepare is absolutely delicious and full of life-giving nutrition. I am amazed at how much nutritious food is out there, be it Indian, Thai, New American, or just my own concoctions. I am not sure if I will ever master it all because there is so much of it to play with, but I'm sure I will have a ton of fun continually trying out new things to eat. :-)

One quick note: The word 'decision' comes from Old French,

which borrowed it from the Latin – decisio. The 'de' etymologically means 'off or down' (dethrone, descend) and the 'cision' comes from the Latin word meaning 'to cut' (think of scissors or incision). So the word 'decision' literally means to cut down or to cut off (other options or arguments), until you are left with only one final choice, and hence, you've made a decision. You cast away all other possible options until there is only one option left…and that's the one you take.

So make a list of things you can do right now that will start you on the path of changing your life immediately. If you have always wanted to exercise – workout, hike, do floor exercises, or whatever – start today and create the new you. It is in your power to take control and begin the future you want. The world has a place for the new you. Will you go there?

> *"Be the change you want to see in the world."*
> ~ Mahatma Gandhi

> *"The mind is the root from which all things grow. If you can understand the mind, everything else is included."*
> ~ Bodhidharma

Be the Person You Want to Become

You have to 'be' what you want to attract, before you can attract what you want into your life.

My wife, Beth, told me a story that exemplifies this perfectly: Two female flight attendants were talking while sitting on the jump seat (Beth being one of them), discussing numerous topics. Then the other woman mentioned she would really like to stop being single, and find a man who enjoyed healthy eating, liked to do outdoor things, was physically in good shape, and was also adventurous. Beth paused, and offered up an explanation that the person she just described would be looking for a partner who also had those personal characteristics and actually lived that lifestyle. And it was obvious that her friend still had a lot of work that needed to be done if she wanted to live this described lifestyle herself and attract someone who also appreciated these same traits.

This single woman took the advice to heart, changed her diet, started doing more outdoor activities, and became what she wanted to become in the futuristic vision of herself. Shortly thereafter she met the man of her dreams and they did all of these things together. She actually manifested everything she wanted, by first becoming the person she desired to be in the future! Actions matter when you want to manifest, and like attracts like.

Carl Jung described Love as being the highest form of self-admiration. By this, I think he meant that if I admire certain things in me, and I see them in you, I say: "Wow, you are so cool! I love everything about you!"

What works is to envision the life you want to have and start living it. Then you will *be* your future self now, attract all that you want, and enjoy everything now as well as long into the future.

I once received a phone call from someone close to me who was going through a major break-up of her romantic relationship, was extremely distraught, and in tears. After listening to the details of the situation, I asked her what she would like to do in the future, possibly something she did previously that she hadn't done since she got involved in this (now defunct) relationship.

Her first response was that she didn't know and couldn't think of anything. I asked her "What if you did know? What would that look like?" After giving it some thought, she said that she has always liked sewing, and she use to sew a lot before the relationship, but with the time it takes and not having the space needed, it was all but impossible to continue her craft after moving in and combining households.

I asked her if she would have an area to set up her sewing room when she moved back to the house she owned and had rented on a monthly basis to someone else. She said "Yes. I don't need the extra bedroom anymore because my daughter is grown and has moved out, and that would make a really great sewing room!" She continued to explain how perfect that set up would be and that she could have one of her girlfriends come over that also liked sewing and they could make all kinds of things, on and on and on, until she could hardly wait to complete the move and get into her new future. "Wow, things are going to be so great! There's so much I stopped doing that I really miss!"

The end of the conversation was nothing like the beginning. A little bit of vision, a plan for the future, and how to get there, goes a long way in lifting our spirits. We all manifest by seeing, hearing, or feeling our way into the future we want to create.

Creation is active participation. You have the ability to learn everything you need to learn, and when you do, you will attract those individuals into your life who are on similar paths and seeking similar outcomes. By choosing your path, projecting your intentions from your Spiritual Center, and then taking the actions needed, you bring everything you want into your life.

> *"We are what we do. Excellence, therefore, is not an act, but a habit."*
>
> ~ Aristotle

> *"On the one hand, the individual unit is lost in number, on the other it is torn apart in the collectivity, and in yet a third direction it stretches out in becoming."*
>
> ~ Pierre Teilhard de Chardin

Reflecting on this chapter, I invite you to write down any applicable thoughts, take-aways, or lightbulb moments that your inner-self is realizing and trying to communicate to you:

_____

_____

_____

_____

_____

_____

_____

_____

_____

_____

_____

Final Thoughts

Joseph Campbell was asked in an interview for *The Power of Myth with Bill Moyers*, if he took the Bible literally or metaphorically. He answered that you'd have to take it metaphorically, because if you took it literally it doesn't make any sense, like in the case of the crucifixion where it is said Christ bodily rose to heaven – then where did he go? Heaven doesn't exist in the physical realm; it's not a place you can physically travel to. It doesn't exist in time or space, it's beyond time and space.

Then he gave the best explanation of the crucifixion I have ever heard. He explained it metaphorically as Christ ascending from the lower animalistic nature of man to the higher, more evolved spiritual nature of mankind. Then he said it wasn't even about Christ! The real metaphor is referring to YOU! Have YOU transitioned from your lower mundane animalistic nature to the higher enlightened spiritual reality that is waiting for you to experience?

Manifesting into who we are meant to become is our task.

There was a time when I didn't know how to manifest the relationship I wanted to have. There was also a time when I didn't know how to create wealth and abundance. There was even a time when I didn't know how to ride a bicycle. But I took the time to learn what I would need to know in order to manifest the things I wanted. I also increasingly developed my spirituality and this lets me manifest the outcomes that I want in ways I had never thought possible.

You can increasingly evolve your spirituality by practicing the various forms of meditation mentioned earlier. By doing this you will become proficient at projecting your intentions to the Collective Subconscious and Universal Unconscious from your Spiritual Center. This will bring about the future you wish to manifest. It just takes your active participation.

It is my sincere hope that you will take this journey, and once you have accomplished everything you desire, you help others to do the same by sharing this knowledge.

It's only through introspection, and the spreading of love and kindness, that the world can be made better.

Through kindness comes discovery; through love comes freedom and authenticity.

Appendix

You can build the following spreadsheet in Excel® and have your data entries automatically calculate the other cells as needed. Once you have a working blank spreadsheet, you can enter the pertinent information for each property you are considering and save them separately under that property's address, and retain the blank form for future analysis. This will give you a good idea of the market, as well as finalizing any decisions on the properties you're interested in.

Financial Analysis Property Address				
Purchase Price			0	
Inside Closing Costs	0			
3rd Party Closing Costs	0			
Prepaids	0			
Total Closing Costs			0	
Total Purchase Price & Closing Costs				0
Purchase Price		0		
Less Down Payment		0		
Loan Amount				0
Down Payment		0		
Plus Closing Costs		0		
Cash to Close				0

Profitability	Current		Pro Forma	
Income/Month		0		0
P&I (principle & interest - Monthly)	0		0	
Taxes/Month	0		0	
Insurance/Month	0		0	
Trash, Water, Sewer, Lawn/Month	0		0	
Total Expenses/Month		0		0
Gross Profit/Month		0		0
Gross Profit/Year		0		0
Mortgage Buy Down - Year 1		0		0
Total without Appreciation		0		0
5% Appreciation on Purchase Price		0		0
Total Wealth Accumulation - Year 1		0		0
Capitalization Rate (Cap Rate)		0.00%		0.00%
Gross Rent Multiplier (GRM)		0.00%		0.00%

Action Steps I Promise Myself to Take, Practice, and Then Master

1. _____

2. _____

3. _____

4. _____

5. _____

6. _____

7. _____

8. _____

9. _____

10. _____

11. _____

12. _____

My Five Year Plan

One Year Goals

1. _____

2. _____

3. _____

4. _____

5. _____

Two Year Goals

1. _____

2. _____

3. _____

4. _____

5. _____

Three Year Goals

1. _____
2. _____
3. _____
4. _____
5. _____

Four Year Goals

1. _____
2. _____
3. _____
4. _____
5. _____

Five Year Goals

1. _____
2. _____
3. _____
4. _____
5. _____

I look forward to hearing from you. Please send your comments and feedback to: ManifestYourFutureDesign.Life@gmail.com

Thank You,
Dennis A. Belanger